THE SIMPLE WILL IN OHIO

THE SIMPLE WILL
IN OHIO

MARILYN J. MAAG

Strauss & Troy
Cincinnati, Ohio

NDERSON'S OHIO PRACTICE MANUAL SERIES

CONTENTS

INTRODUCTION

The Simple Will Handbook is a concise practice manual created to take the attorney through the step-by-step process of drafting, executing, and amending a simple Will. The Handbook explains how the attorney determines whether a simple Will is appropriate for a particular client. The Handbook also explains the law related to drafting a simple Will. The information in the Handbook is organized by headings and subheadings and carefully indexed to enable the attorney to find answers quickly to the legal and practical questions that arise when drafting a simple Will.

The Handbook includes form documents, as well as numerous form provisions. Thus, the attorney can use the basic Will form included in the Handbook to draft a Will, modifying it with the various specific provisions as appropriate.

The Handbook is written clearly and concisely. Attorneys who do not regularly practice in the estate planning area can easily find answers to their questions and practical guidance when they draft, execute, and amend simple Wills.

CHAPTER 1

Preliminary Considerations

1.1 Deciding When to Use a Simple Will

A simple Will is a Will that does not include trust provisions within the Will and does not pour assets into a trust that was created during the testator's life. Determining whether a simple Will is an appropriate estate planning device involves considering whether a more complex estate plan is necessary. A simple Will is used when there is no tax or other reason to hold the testator's assets in a trust after the testator's death.

During the first interview with the client about his or her estate plan, the attorney should gather information about the client's goals and intentions and determine whether the client wants to create a trust. There are many reasons to create a trust, such as the following:

(1) The client may want to hold assets for the client's children until they reach certain ages.[1]

(2) The client may want to create a trust for money management reasons. The trust may be funded during the client's lifetime to enable the trustee to manage the client's money for the client. After the client's death, the trustee may manage the trust assets for the surviving spouse and/or children.

(3) The client may want to create a trust to control the disposition of the trust assets after the client's spouse's death. This type of trust is commonly known as a QTIP (qualified terminable interest property) trust.[2]

---

[1] If the client does not create a trust but transfers assets outright to a minor under the Transfers to Minors Act (R.C. §§ 1339.31–1339.39), then the custodian must pay over the assets to the minor when the minor reaches age twenty-one.

[2] *See* I.R.C. § 2056(b)(7)(B). Qualified terminable interest property is property that passes from the decedent, in which the surviving spouse has a life income

1

(4) The client may want to create a trust to provide for a disabled or incompetent family member.

(5) If assets of the client and his or her spouse, if any, exceed $600,000 in value, then the client and his or her spouse may want to create trusts to preserve both spouses' unified credits[3] against federal gift and estate tax. Credit shelter trusts are discussed further in Section 1.2.

(6) The client may want to create a trust to hold assets that are exempt from generation-skipping transfer tax.[4]

Some of the reasons for creating a trust are not related to avoiding taxes. During the interview with the client, the attorney must listen to the client's concerns about family members and determine whether the client has personal, non-tax-related reasons to create a trust.

Additionally, the client should complete an Estate Planning Questionnaire (Appendix, Forms A and B) listing the items of property owned by the client, the form of ownership (such as sole ownership or joint ownership with the right of survivorship), and the value of the items of property. The attorney should use the information on the Estate Planning Questionnaire to determine whether the client should consider creating a trust or trusts for tax reasons. When the attorney is planning the estates of a married couple, the attorney should look carefully at the Estate Planning Questionnaire to determine whether the couple owns more than $600,000 of property and, if so, whether credit shelter trusts[5] are an appropriate estate planning device.

interest, and as to which an election has been made to treat the property as qualified terminable interest property. The surviving spouse has a "qualifying" life income interest if the surviving spouse is entitled to all income from the property, payable annually or more frequently, and no one may appoint any part of the property to any person other than the surviving spouse. I.R.C. § 2056(b)(7)(B)(ii).

[3] Section 2010 of the Internal Revenue Code states that the estate of every decedent has a credit of $192,800.

[4] *See* I.R.C. § 2601 *et seq.* The generation-skipping transfer tax is imposed, very simply stated, on transfers from grandparents to grandchildren that skip estate taxation in the children's estates. Each person has a $1 million exemption from generation-skipping tax, meaning that a grandparent may transfer up to $1 million to his or her grandchildren before generation-skipping tax is imposed. When generation-skipping tax is imposed, however, it is imposed at the highest estate tax rate, which is 55% currently.

[5] Credit shelter trusts are explained in Section 1.2 of this Chapter.

If there is no tax-related or personal, non-tax-related reason for the client to create a trust, then the attorney should recommend a simple Will. Examples of Will provisions and explanations of issues to consider are included in the following chapters.

1.2 Using Credit Shelter Trusts for Married Couples With More Than $600,000 of Property

The federal gift and estate tax credit is $192,800 for persons dying in 1987 and thereafter.[6] Using this credit, the decedent may transfer $600,000 of property free of federal gift and estate tax. The credit is applied to gifts made during the decedent's lifetime and to transfers made at his or her death.[7]

"Credit Shelter Trusts" often are used by married couples to ensure that both spouses' unified credits are used to transfer property. If both spouses use their unified credits, the couple may transfer a total of $1,200,000 to their children (or to whomever they want to give their property) free of federal gift and estate tax. Without the use of Credit Shelter Trusts, the unified credit of the first spouse to die frequently is not used.

Assume, for example, that Husband and Wife sign simple Wills, leaving everything to each other, and Wife dies first. All of Wife's property then is transferred to Husband free of federal gift and estate tax because of the marital deduction.[8] When Husband dies years later, he has a unified credit of $600,000, meaning that he may transfer $600,000 of property free of federal gift and estate tax. If his estate is worth more than $600,000, then he must pay taxes on the excess amount. In this example, the married couple used only Husband's unified credit and lost Wife's. This result may be avoided through the use of Credit Shelter Trusts.

A Credit Shelter Trust divides the trust assets into two funds, often called the Marital Trust and the Family Trust. The Family Trust is funded first with $600,000. The Family Trust usually is

---

[6] I.R.C. § 2010.

[7] *See* I.R.C. §§ 2010 and 2012.

[8] Under current tax laws, there is an unlimited marital deduction, meaning that transfers between spouses are not subject to federal gift and estate tax. I.R.C. § 2056.

held for the surviving spouse's benefit[9] during his or her lifetime and distributed to the children and grandchildren (or other beneficiaries) upon the surviving spouse's death. The purpose of the Family Trust is to preserve the Settlor's unified credit by setting aside $600,000 of property to be transferred to the Settlor's children and grandchildren (or other beneficiaries).

If the Settlor owns property in excess of $600,000, the excess amount is distributed outright to the surviving spouse or held in the Marital Trust for the surviving spouse's benefit. The assets that are transferred to the surviving spouse, either outright or in the Marital Trust, are transferred free of federal gift and estate tax because of the marital deduction.[10]

Through the use of Credit Shelter Trusts, a married couple ensures that the first spouse to die will use his or her unified credit. All assets not transferred under the unified credit will be transferred to the surviving spouse under the marital deduction. As a result, no estate tax is due upon the death of the first spouse. Credit Shelter Trusts permit both spouses to use their unified credits as well as ensure that the surviving spouse's support, maintenance, and medical needs will be taken care of after the first spouse dies.

---

[9] The spouse may receive all income earned by the Family Trust and principal in the trustee's discretion. Additionally, the Settlor may give the spouse the right to withdraw the greater of $5,000 or 5% of the trust principal, as determined on the last day of the calendar year. *See* I.R.C. § 2041(b)(2). The Settlor may give the spouse significant benefits from the Family Trust to ensure that the spouse will receive money for support and medical care, if necessary, but should not give the spouse so much control over the Family Trust or so many benefits from the Family Trust as to include the Family Trust in the spouse's estate. *See* I.R.C. §§ 2035 (transfer of life insurance within three years of death), 2036 (retained life interest), 2037 (reversionary interest), 2038 (power to revoke), and 2041 (powers of appointment).

[10] I.R.C. § 2056.

CHAPTER 2

Dispositive Provisions

2.1 Generally

A Will should be written clearly and concisely so that the testator signs the Will with confidence that he or she understands the Will. A Will generally is divided into three sections: the dispositive provisions, the provisions appointing the Executor and the other fiduciaries, and the provisions describing the fiduciaries' powers.

The dispositive provisions state how the testator's property is to be divided. Specific bequests should be stated first, followed by directions about the transfer of the residue. The residuary clause in a Will disposes of that portion of the testator's property that remains after the debts have been paid and the specific bequests have been satisfied. Property is transferred according to the residuary clause in a Will if the property is not expressly disposed of by other provisions of the Will.

Bequest of Tangibles

2.2 —In the Will

Tangible personal property is corporeal, material, and capable of being touched. Examples of tangible personal property are automobiles, household furnishings, books, clothing and jewelry.

Clients frequently want to make specific bequests of tangible personal property to certain beneficiaries. The specific bequest should describe the property precisely, so that the Executor has no doubt about which item of property is bequested. Many items of personal property, such as jewelry, are very similar.

The following are examples of specific bequests:

Example 1. I give my antique doll to my niece, * , if she survives me by 30 days. If * does not so survive me, then this bequest shall lapse and my Executor shall transfer my antique doll with the residue of my estate.

Example 2. I give $25,000 to my friend, * , if he survives me by 30 days. If he does not so survive me, I make this bequest to his then living lineal descendants, per stirpes.

Example 3. I give my engagement ring, which is a gold ring with one large diamond and several smaller diamonds and rubies on it, to my daughter, * , if she survives me by 30 days. If she does not so survive me, I give my engagement ring to my son, * , if he survives me by 30 days.

The Will should state who will receive the bequest if the named beneficiary does not survive the testator. If the testator wants the bequest to lapse and wants the Executor to distribute the bequested property to the residual beneficiaries, then the Will should state this expressly (as in the examples above). Ohio Revised Code § 2107.52, Ohio's anti-lapse statute, states that when the testator devises real or personal property to a relative of the testator and the relative dies, leaving lineal descendants surviving him or her, the lineal descendants of the devisee take the property. If the testator does not want the anti-lapse statute to apply, then the testator should state his or her intent clearly in the Will.

A client may want to give all of his or her tangible personal property to one person, such as a spouse, or in shares (equal or otherwise) to a group of people, such as his or her children. See the discussion in Section 2.9 of this Chapter regarding bequests to lineal descendants "per stirpes" or "per capita." The following provision gives the tangible personal property to the surviving spouse or, in the alternative, to the testator's children:

I give to my spouse, * , if he survives me by 30 days, all of my tangible personal property, such as, but not limited to, automobiles, household furnishings and decorations, books, paintings, clothing, and jewelry. If my spouse does not survive me by 30 days, I give my tangible personal property to my children who survive me by 30 days. My children shall divide my tangible personal property among themselves as nearly equally as possible. If my children are unable to agree, my Executor shall divide my tangible personal property among my children as nearly equally as possible.

2.3 —In a Letter

An alternative to making specific bequests in a Will is to prepare a letter, which is addressed to the Executor or beneficiaries and signed by the testator, stating how the tangible personal property is to be divided. Under Ohio law, this letter must exist at the time the Will is signed.[1] A Will may not incorporate by reference a document that is not in existence at the time the Will is signed.

2.4 Bequest of Real Property

The attorney should look at the deed to any real property owned by the client to determine the form of ownership. If the client is the sole owner, then he or she may state in his or her Will how the real property will be transferred. If the client owns the property jointly with another person with the right of survivorship, then the property is transferred to the surviving owner upon the client's death. If the client is a co-owner of the property with another person or persons, then the client may transfer only his or her interest, which will be a percentage of the entire interest, in his or her Will. It is important to note that real property held jointly with the right of survivorship is transferred automatically to the surviving owner and is not transferred under the Will.[2]

Because real property frequently is subject to a mortgage, the Will should state whether the Executor should pay the mortgage in full or in part. The testator may want to give the Executor the

---

[1] R.C. § 2107.05.

[2] *See* 19 Ohio Jur. 3d *Cotenancy and Partition* § 3 (1980); 1 Anderson's Ohio Probate Practice and Procedure § 16.09 (1990).

flexibility to decide whether to pay the mortgage. Such flexibility often is a good idea because the circumstances that the Executor and the beneficiaries will face are unknown at the time the testator creates the Will. An example giving such flexibility is included below.

The following are examples of provisions transferring real property:

> **Example 1.** I give any real property that I may own at the time of my death, including buildings, fixtures, and appurtenances located on the real property and all insurance policies relating to the real property, to my spouse, * , if she survives me by 30 days. If my spouse does not so survive me, this devise shall lapse.

> **Example 2.** I give to my spouse, * , if she survives me by 30 days, any interest I may have in any residential real property at the time of my death, subject to any mortgage on the real property. If my spouse does not so survive me, this devise shall lapse.

> **Example 3.** I give to my spouse, * , if he survives me by 30 days, any interest I may have in any residential real property at the time of my death, subject to any mortgage on the real property, provided that my Executor may decide, in my Executor's sole discretion, to pay the mortgage in full or in part. If my spouse does not so survive me, this devise shall lapse.

2.5   Bequest of Securities

A testator may give a certain number of shares of stock (a general bequest) or a testator may identify the specific shares that he or she is giving (a specific bequest). The distinction between these types of gifts is seen in the examples below.

General Bequest of Securities

I give to * , if he survives me by 30 days, one hundred shares of the common stock of ABC Corporation.

Specific Bequest of Securities

I give to * , if he survives me by 30 days, all the shares of the common stock of ABC Corporation held by me at my death.

This bequest shall consist of the one hundred shares of the common stock of ABC Corporation that I own presently, which may increase or decrease in number due to corporate mergers, consolidations, or reorganizations, stock splits or stock dividends. If at the time of my death the one hundred shares of common stock that I own presently have decreased in number, then this bequest is limited to the number of shares I actually own at the time of my death.

2.6 General and Specific Legacies

A "legacy" is a disposition of real or personal property; the term is used interchangeably with the term "bequest."[3] Although the term "devise" technically refers to a gift of real property, it has been used interchangeably in some instances with the term "bequest."[4]

A "general legacy" is a bequest, such as a bequest of a sum of money, that is paid out of the general assets of an estate.[5] A "specific legacy" is paid out of a specified source.[6] The distinction between these types of legacies is seen in the examples below.

General Legacy
I give to my housekeeper, * , the sum of Five Thousand Dollars ($5,000.00), if she survives me by 30 days, in gratitude for her many years of assistance. If she does not so survive me, then this bequest shall lapse.

Specific Legacy
I give to my housekeeper, * , the sum of Five Thousand Dollars

---

[3] 32 OHIO JUR. 3d *Decedents' Estates* § 769 (1981).

[4] *See* Donnelly v. Baughman, 4 Ohio L. Abs. 51 (App. 1925); Park Nat'l Bank v. Dillon, 82 Ohio L. Abs. 387, 165 N.E.2d 829 (C.P. 1959); 32 OHIO JUR. 3d *Decedents' Estates* § 769 (1981).

[5] Holmes v. Hrobon, 158 Ohio St. 508, 49 Ohio Op. 450, 110 N.E.2d 574 (1953); Collins v. Patton, 64 Ohio L. Abs. 518, 113 N.E.2d 100 (App. 1952); Varner v. French, 12 Ohio L. Abs. 609 (App. 1932); In re Mellot's Estate, 50 Ohio Op. 517, 65 Ohio L. Abs. 182, 113 N.E.2d 780 (1953), *aff'd*, 162 Ohio St. 113, 54 Ohio Op. 53, 121 N.E.2d 7 (1954); Rote v. Warner, 17 Ohio C.C. 342, 9 Ohio Cir. Dec. 536, *aff'd*, 57 Ohio St. 633, 50 N.E. 1133 (1897).

[6] In re Estate of Radu, 35 Ohio App. 2d 187, 64 Ohio Op. 2d 293, 301 N.E.2d 263 (1973); Collins v. Patton, 64 Ohio L. Abs. 518, 113 N.E.2d 100 (App. 1952); Shaw v. Shaw, 32 Ohio App. 168, 167 N.E. 611 (1928); Warren v. Shoemaker, 4 Ohio Misc. 15, 33 Ohio Op. 2d 20, 207 N.E.2d 419 (P. Ct. 1965).

($5,000.00), if she survives me by 30 days, to be paid from my money market fund in * Bank (account number _____) or from the residue of my estate if I do not own the account at the time of my death or if there are not sufficient funds in the account at the time of my death. If she does not so survive me, then this bequest shall lapse.

2.7 Disposition of Residue

The "residue" of an estate is the balance left after the debts of the estate and all bequests have been paid.[7] The residual clause usually follows the other dispositive provisions of the Will. Frequently, a testator will want to give the residue of his or her estate to his or her children and to the children (the testator's grandchildren) of a deceased child. Children and grandchildren (and more distant generations of blood relatives) are most precisely referred to as "lineal descendants." The distribution among the children and grandchildren may be made "per stirpes" or "per capita." A gift of the residue of the testator's estate to the testator's "then living lineal descendants, per stirpes" is very common. See the discussion in Section 2.9 of this Chapter regarding a gift of the residue to the testator's lineal descendants "per stirpes" or "per capita." An example of a residual clause is as follows:

I give the residue of my estate to my spouse, * , if she survives me by 30 days. If she does not so survive me, I give the residue of my estate to my then living lineal descendants, per stirpes. If neither my spouse nor any lineal descendant of mine survives me by 30 days, I give the residue of my estate to the person(s) who would be entitled to receive it according to the Ohio statute of descent and distribution.

Designation of Beneficiaries

2.8 —Defining Class Membership

A bequest may be made to persons who fit a general description or are members of a class, such as children, grandchildren, or

---

[7] Forsythe v. Mintier, 39 Ohio St. 349 (1883); Huffman v. Berry, 15 Ohio App. 372 (1921); 32 OHIO JUR. 3d *Decedents' Estates* § 786 (1981).

lineal descendants. Generally, membership in a class is determined as of the date the bequest takes effect.[8] Assuming that the testator wants a bequest to take effect at his or her death or shortly thereafter, the Will should state clearly when the class closes. The Will should make references to classes using language such as "then living lineal descendants," meaning all lineal descendants of the testator who are living at the time of the testator's death, or "children who survive me by 30 days."

2.9 —"Per Stirpes" Versus "Per Capita"

Frequently, a testator will want to make a bequest, oftentimes of the residue of the testator's estate, to his or her children and to the children (the testator's grandchildren) of a deceased child. Children and grandchildren (and more distant generations of blood relatives) are most precisely referred to as "lineal descendants." The distribution among the children and grandchildren may be made "per stirpes" or "per capita."

A distribution "per stirpes" means that if a child of the testator is deceased, then the deceased child's share is divided equally among his or her children.[9] Thus, the testator's children, who are more closely related to the testator, will receive larger shares than the testator's grandchildren, who are receiving shares only because their mother or father (the testator's child) has died.

A distribution "per capita" means that if a child of the testator is deceased, then the children of the deceased child, as well as the testator's surviving children, share equally in the testator's estate.[10]

A bequest, oftentimes of the residue of the testator's estate, to the testator's "then living lineal descendants, per stirpes," is very common. Many people perceive a per stirpital distribution as more fair than a per capita distribution because where there is a per capita distribution, certain grandchildren are treated as favorably as children.

[8] *See, e.g.,* Provident Savings Bank & Trust Co. v. Nash, 75 Ohio App. 493, 31 Ohio Op. 290, 62 N.E.2d 736 (1945). *But see* Central Trust Co., N.A. v. Smith, 50 Ohio St. 3d 133, 553 N.E.2d 265 (1990) (holding that class in testamentary trust does not necessarily close at death of testator, but may remain open to enlargement under certain circumstances).

[9] 31 Oнio Jur. 3d *Decedents' Estates* §§ 105, 106 (1981).

[10] *Id.*

2.10 —Defining Stepchildren as "Children"

If the testator wants to include his or her stepchildren as equal beneficiaries with his or her biological or adopted children, then the testator should expressly define the word "child" or "children" to include stepchildren. It is good practice to name the stepchildren to make it clear that they are beneficiaries. For example:

> For all purposes of this Will and the disposition of my estate hereunder, the word "child" or "children" includes my spouse's children by a prior marriage, * and *.

If a testator has stepchildren, but does not intend to make them beneficiaries under his or her Will, then the testator should consider including in the Will a provision similar to the following:

> For all purposes of this Will and the disposition of my estate hereunder, the word "child" or "children" does not include my spouse's children by a prior marriage.

CHAPTER 3

Nomination of Fiduciaries

3.1 Types of Fiduciaries: "Executor" and "Administrator"

The fiduciary who administers an estate is a representative of the decedent, who also acts as a trustee for the beneficiaries and the creditors. There are several different types of fiduciaries who may serve in the administration of a decedent's estate. An executor is a fiduciary named by the testator in his or her Will and appointed under R.C. § 2113.05.[1] If an executor is not named in a Will or if none of the persons named are willing or able to serve, then the probate court must appoint an administrator with the Will annexed.[2]

The term "administrator" refers to a fiduciary who is selected and appointed by the probate court rather than named in the decedent's Will.[3] An administrator de bonis non is a successor fiduciary appointed because the initial fiduciary died without fully administering the estate.[4] In a testate estate, the technical title of the successor fiduciary is the administrator de bonis non with the Will annexed.[5]

Section 2113.15 of the Ohio Revised Code states that the probate court may appoint a special administrator when for some reason there is a delay in the appointment of the executor or administrator and a special administrator is needed to collect and preserve the

[1] 32 OHIO JUR. 3d *Decedents' Estates* § 990 (1981).
[2] R.C. §§ 2113.05 and 2113.12.
[3] 32 OHIO JUR. 3d *Decedents' Estates* § 990 (1981).
[4] R.C. § 2113.19.
[5] 1 ANDERSON'S OHIO PROBATE PRACTICE AND PROCECURE § 10.01 (1990).

decedent's assets and debts during the interim period until the executor or administrator is appointed.

3.2 Qualifications of Executor

A person must meet certain requirements to serve as Executor. The person must be at least eighteen years old to serve as Executor, and must meet the residency requirements.[6] Section 2109.21 states the residency requirements for Executors in Ohio: an adult resident of Ohio may serve; a non-resident may serve if he or she is related to the testator by blood or marriage or if the nominee's state of residence permits a non-resident non-relative to serve as Executor. Administrators, on the other hand, must be residents of the State of Ohio.[7]

The Ohio Revised Code imposes a special requirement for corporate fiduciaries, such as banks and trust companies. Under R.C. § 1109.08, a corporation may serve as executor or administrator only if the corporation has trust powers.

3.3 Bond

A fiduciary must give bond before accepting his or her fiduciary duties,[8] unless a testator requests that the person nominated serve as Executor without bond. The probate court will honor the testator's request that the Executor serve without bond unless the court decides that bond is necessary because of special circumstances.[9]

3.4 Nomination of Successor

A testator generally should nominate more than one person to serve as Executor. If the first person nominated is unwilling to serve or is appointed but resigns, becomes incompetent, or dies, then the next person nominated may serve. Two or more persons may serve as Co-Executors, in which case they must make decisions

[6] *Id.* § 10.02.

[7] R.C. § 2113.06.

[8] R.C. § 2109.04. The court fixes the bond; the minimum amount of the bond is twice the value of personal property plus annual real estate rentals. R.C. § 2109.04(A)(1).

[9] R.C. § 2109.04(A)(2).

by consensus. The signatures of all of the Executors are required on documents. In spite of the inconvenience of more than one Executor, many people choose Co-Executors to provide diversity. For example, if a bank and the surviving spouse act as Co-Executors, then the bank offers its expertise in estate administration and investments, while the surviving spouse offers knowledge of and relationships with the family members/beneficiaries.

3.5   Effect of Divorce on Nomination of Fiduciaries

Section 2107.33 of the Ohio Revised Code states that when a testator is divorced, or separates from a spouse and enters a separation agreement intended to settle the prospective rights of the former spouses in each other's property, and the testator's former spouse is included in the testator's Will, then the testator's Will is amended by operation of law. A transfer of property to the former spouse made in the Will or a grant of a power of appointment to the former spouse is revoked. If the former spouse is nominated as executor, trustee, and/or guardian, then these provisions also are revoked. Property then is transferred under the Will as if the former spouse failed to survive the decedent. Provisions in the Will granting the former spouse a power of appointment or selecting the former spouse to serve as a fiduciary are interpreted as if the former spouse failed to survive the decedent.

3.6   Sample Provisions Naming Executor

The following are examples of provisions naming an Executor:

Example 1. I name *, who resides in Columbus, Ohio, as the Executor of my Will and I direct that she shall serve without bond.

Example 2. I name as the Executor of my Will the first person of the following who is willing and able to serve. I direct that no bond be required of any of them for serving as Executor:

    1. *
    2. *
    3. *

When a bank or trust company is named as Executor of a Will, the nomination should include the successors or assigns of the bank or trust company because the corporation may change its corporate form and/or corporate name in the future. An example of such a nomination is as follows:

> I name * Bank, of Toledo, Ohio, or its successors or assigns, as the Executor of my Will and I direct that it shall serve without bond.

3.7 Nomination of Guardian of Minor Children

Section 2111.12 of the Revised Code states that a parent may in his or her Will appoint a guardian for his or her children, including children who are not born at the time the Will is executed. The testator should name one or more successor guardians, in case the first person nominated is unwilling or unable to serve. An example of a guardian nomination provision is as follows:

> I request that the court of proper jurisdiction appoint as Guardian of the person and estate of any minor child of mine who survives me the first-named one of the following who can and will qualify to serve, and if the one qualifying ceases to serve for any reason, the next in the order named who can and will qualify to serve. I direct that no bond be required of any of them for serving as Guardian:
>
> 1. _____
> 2. _____
> 3. _____

CHAPTER 4

Powers of Executor

4.1 Duties of Executor

An Executor has various duties prescribed by the Ohio Probate Code, including the duties to collect the assets,[1] file an inventory,[2] pay debts and taxes,[3] distribute the property as directed in the Will,[4] and file accounts with the probate court.[5] The Executor must perform his or her duties in good faith and with the degree of care that an ordinary person shows in handling his or her own business.[6]

4.2 Sale of Real or Personal Property

An Executor who is authorized by Will to sell real or personal property may do so without a court order.[7] An Executor with the authority to sell may do so whenever the Executor decides the sale is in the best interest of the estate, unless the Will limits the Executor's authority in some way.[8]

If the Will does not authorize the Executor to sell personal property, then the probate court must authorize a sale, as stated in R.C. §§ 2113.40–2113.44. If the Will does not authorize the Executor to sell real property, then, as provided in R.C. § 2127.01, Chapter 2127 governs a sale of real property. To give the Executor the

[1] R.C. §§ 2113.25–2113.28.
[2] R.C. §§ 2115.01–2115.17.
[3] R.C. §§ 2113.86; 2117.01–2117.42.
[4] R.C. §§ 2113.51–2113.59.
[5] R.C. §§ 2113.31–2113.38.
[6] 33 OHIO JUR. 3d *Decedents' Estates* § 1490 (1982).
[7] R.C. § 2113.39.
[8] *Id.*

17

freedom to sell personal and/or real property whenever the Executor decides that the sale is in the best interest of the estate,[9] the Will should give the Executor the specific authority to sell property. Examples of such provisions are as follows:

> **Example 1.** I give the Executor of my estate the authority to sell, rent, lease, mortgage, pledge, repair, improve, or convey any real or personal property upon the terms, including price, that my Executor decides are in the best interest of my estate.

> **Example 2.** I direct my Executor to sell my home located at _____ and to distribute the proceeds of the sale with the residue of my estate.

> **Example 3.** I authorize my Executor to sell any real or personal property at a public or private sale, for cash or on credit, and upon the terms, including price, that my Executor decides are in the best interest of my estate.

4.3 Investments

An Executor's investment choices are limited by the provisions of Section 2109.37 of the Revised Code, unless the Will states otherwise or the probate court authorizes the Executor to make specific investments. The testator may want to authorize the Executor to retain the investments that are part of the estate at the time of the testator's death, as in the following example:

> I authorize the Executor of my estate to retain the investments that are part of my estate at the time of my death, regardless of whether the investments are authorized by the statutes governing investments of fiduciaries, if my Executor decides in good faith that retention of the investments is in the best interest of my estate.

The testator also may direct specifically that the Executor may not sell certain investments.

Finally, the testator may give the Executor the freedom to retain investments, or sell them and reinvest the proceeds, all as the Executor sees fit, as in the following example:

> I authorize the Executor of my estate to retain the investments

---

[9] 1 ANDERSON'S OHIO PROBATE PRACTICE AND PROCEDURE § 19.01 (1990).

that are part of my estate at the time of my death, regardless
of whether the investments are authorized by the statutes governing investments of fiduciaries, if my Executor decides in good
faith that retention of the investments is in the best interest of
my estate. My Executor may sell investments as my Executor
sees fit and my Executor may invest and reinvest in whatever
property my Executor decides is reasonable, regardless of statutory authorization, including in a common trust fund for the
investment of fiduciary funds.

4.4   Continuing the Decedent's Business

An Executor may, without personal liability for losses incurred,
continue the decedent's business for one month after the Executor's
appointment, unless the probate court decides otherwise.[10] The court
may authorize the Executor to continue the decedent's business for
a longer period of time, but only after giving notice to the surviving
spouse and the distributees and holding a hearing on the issue.[11]
The Executor must file monthly reports to the court during the
time period that the Executor is continuing the decedent's business.[12]

A testator may give his or her Executor authorization to continue
a business, without probate court approval and without reporting
to the probate court, by giving the Executor this power in the Will.
The testator may include within this power the authority to liquidate
and/or to sell the business, as in the folllowing example:

> I authorize the Executor of my estate to continue to operate
> any business interest I may own at the time of my death, for the
> time period that my Executor decides is appropriate. My Executor
> shall not be personally liable for losses resulting from my Exe-
> cutor's operation of my business. I waive any requirement that
> my Executor report to the probate court regarding the operation
> of my business. Additionally, my Executor may liquidate or sell
> my business at the time and under the terms and conditions that
> my Executor decides are best. I give my Executor the additional
> powers that may be necessary for my Executor to operate or sell

[10] R.C. § 2113.30.
[11] *Id.*
[12] *Id.*

my business interest, including the power to borrow money for business reasons, to encumber business assets, and to employ managers and employees that my Executor decides are necessary to continue operation of the business.

A testator may authorize his or her Executor to continue an interest in a particular business for a specified period of time, as in the following example:

> I authorize my Executor, in my Executor's sole discretion, to continue any interest I may own in * Partnership at the time of my death. I authorize my Executor to continue my interest in the partnership for no more than _____ years.

4.5 Optional Additional Powers

The testator cannot anticipate and plan for all of the circumstances that will exist at his or her death. The testator cannot project for certain the size of his or her estate, the needs of his or her family, or the condition of his or her business. For these reasons, the testator should consider giving the Executor broad powers to administer and manage the estate. The testator should consider giving the Executor as much flexibility as possible to deal with the circumstances that will exist at the time of the testator's death.

The testator should consider giving the Executor additional powers, such as the power to borrow money; the power to exercise (or not exercise) rights of ownership regarding securities, such as the right to vote; the power to exercise (or not exercise) options to purchase securities; the power to employ agents, such as attorneys and investment advisers; the power to disclaim any interest the testator may have in property; the power to compromise and settle claims in favor of or against the testator's estate upon whatever terms the Executor decides are best; and the power to open a securities brokerage account if the Executor decides this is appropriate.

CHAPTER 5

Additional Drafting Considerations

5.1   Incorporation by Reference

Revised Code § 2107.05 states that a document (or book, record, or memorandum) may be incorporated by reference in a Will, but only if the document actually exists when the Will is signed and the Will refers to the document as an existing document.[1] Furthermore, the document that is incorporated by reference must be filed with the probate court when the Will is filed or within thirty days after the Will is filed.[2] Thus, a person cannot amend his or her Will

---

[1] *See* 31 OHIO JUR. 3d *Decedents' Estates* § 342 (1981).
[2] R.C. § 2107.05.

by a letter or other document that is not created until after the
Will is signed.

5.2 Interest on Bequests

Under R.C. § 2113.531, the beneficiary of a general legacy[3] does
not receive interest on the legacy. If the testator would like the
beneficiary of a general legacy to receive interest, then the testator
should state this intention in the Will. The beneficiary of a specific
legacy,[4] however, receives the interest attributable to that specific
piece of property from the date of death to the date of distribution.[5]

There are two exceptions to the rule that general legacies do not
bear interest: a bequest of money to the surviving spouse or to a
trust. The amount of interest to be distributed to the surviving
spouse is calculated as directed in R.C. § 2109.67. Revised Code §
1340.04(B) applies to accumulated income in an estate passing into
a trust.

The rules regarding interest on bequests must be considered when
the testator is preparing a Will because the testator may want to
alter the general rules, i.e., to provide that a beneficiary of a general
legacy receives interest on the legacy.

5.3 Lapse of Bequests

A bequest to a beneficiary who predeceases the testator, or who
dies within thirty days after the testator,[6] lapses. The bequest may
be preserved if the Will states who will receive the bequest if the
first-named beneficiary predeceases the testator. If the Will does
not name a successor beneficiary, then the anti-lapse statute may
apply to the bequest. Revised Code § 2107.52, the anti-lapse statute,
provides that when a bequest is made to a relative of the testator

---

[3] A general legacy does not involve a specific piece of property. 1 ANDERSON'S
OHIO PROBATE PRACTICE AND PROCEDURE § 21.04 B (1990). For example, a bequest of
a certain amount of money is a general legacy. See the additional discussion in
Section 2.6.

[4] A specific legacy is a gift of a particular, clearly identifiable piece of property.
1 ANDERSON'S OHIO PROBATE PRACTICE AND PROCEDURE § 21.04 B (1990). *See* the
additional discussion in Section 2.6.

[5] R.C. § 2109.67(B)(1).

[6] R.C. § 2105.21.

and the relative predeceases the testator, then the relative's children share the bequest.

When making a Will, the testator should be careful to consider who will receive a bequest if the beneficiary predeceases the testator. For example, the testator may want to give some money to his sister because she had been a close friend to him throughout his life, but the testator may not want to give the money to his sister's children. Thus, in this example, the testator would want the bequest to his sister to lapse if his sister did not survive him; the testator should state this intention in his Will. If the Will contains a residuary clause, then unless the testator states otherwise, the lapsed legacy will pass under the residuary clause.[7]

The following provision is written so that if the testator's sister predeceases him, then his bequest to his sister does not lapse, but is distributed instead to his sister's children, according to the provisions of the anti-lapse statute.

> I give Fifty Thousand Dollars ($50,000.00) to my sister, * , because she has been a close friend to me throughout my life.

If the testator wants the money to go to his brother if his sister does not survive him, then the testator should state this intention clearly, as in the following example:

> I give Fifty Thousand Dollars ($50,000.00) to my sister, * , because she has been a close friend to me throughout my life. If * does not survive me by 30 days, then I make this bequest to my brother, * .

If the testator wants the money to pass with the residue of his estate if his sister does not survive him, then the testator should make this clear by stating that the bequest will lapse and that lapsed and otherwise ineffective transfers will pass with the residue, as illustrated in the following examples:

> **Example 1.** I give Fifty Thousand Dollars ($50,000.00) to my sister, * , because she has been a close friend to me throughout my life. If * does not survive me by 30 days, then this bequest shall lapse.

> **Example 2.** I give the residue of my estate, including any property

---

[7] 32 OHIO JUR. 3d *Decedent's Estates* § 889 (1981).

ineffectively transferred under the other provisions of my Will, in equal shares to my children, * and * .

Rights of Spouse

5.4 —Right to Automobile

Under R.C. § 2106.18, the surviving spouse may select one automobile, which was owned by the deceased spouse, to be the property of the surviving spouse, if the deceased spouse did not give the automobile to someone else by specific bequest in his or her Will.

5.5 —Allowance for Support

The surviving spouse and/or minor children of the decedent are entitled to an allowance for support, distributed in money or property from the estate's assets. The entire allowance for support is distributed to the surviving spouse if:

(a) Only a spouse survives and no minor children of the decedent survive; or

(b) A spouse and minor children of the decedent survive, and all of the surviving minors are children of the surviving spouse.

If, however, a person dies leaving a surviving spouse and minor children, and not all of the minors are children of the decedent and the surviving spouse, the allowance for support is to be equitably divided by the probate court among the surviving spouse and the minors who are not children of the surviving spouse. In making such a division the court is directed to take into consideration the respective needs of the surviving spouse, the minors who are children of the surviving spouse and the decedent, and the minors who are children of the decedent but not of the surviving spouse.

5.6 —Right to Live in "Mansion House"

The surviving spouse may remain in the "mansion house,"[8] which is the home that the decedent and the surviving spouse had shared,

---

[8] "Mansion house" is defined in R.C. § 2106.16(A) to include the decedent's interest in the parcel of land on which the house is situated, lots or farm land adjacent to the house and used with it as the home of the decedent, and the decedent's interest in the household goods contained in the house.

rent-free for one year.[9] If the Executor must sell the house to pay the decedent's debts, then the surviving spouse is entitled to compensation in the amount of the fair market value of the use of the mansion house for the unexpired one-year term.[10]

5.7 —Right to Take Against Will

The surviving spouse may take under the Will or take under R. C. § 2105.06, Ohio's statute of descent and distribution. The surviving spouse electing to take under the statute receives one-half of the net estate unless two or more of the decedent's children, or their lineal descendants survive, in which case the surviving spouse receives one-third of the net estate under Division (C) of R.C. § 2106.01. The allowance for support is deducted from the gross estate in arriving at the net estate.[11] The net estate does not include the value of an automobile selected by the surviving spouse pursuant to R.C. § 2106.18.[12]

If the surviving spouse elects to take the statutory share rather than the testamentary share, the surviving spouse, under R.C. § 2106.01, is entitled to elect to take the decedent's interest in the mansion house as part or all of the statutory share, provided that the statutory share is equal to or greater than the decedent's interest in the mansion house as determined under the provisions of R.C. § 2106.10.

5.8 —Right To Purchase Mansion House and Other Property

Pursuant to R.C. § 2106.16, the surviving spouse, even though also acting as the fiduciary, may purchase the mansion house at its appraised value if the mansion house is not specifically bequeathed. The surviving spouse may purchase the mansion house at the appraised value, which insulates the surviving spouse from competing with other purchasers in the marketplace. Section 2106.16(B) states that the surviving spouse may purchase any other

[9] R.C. § 2106.15.
[10] *Id.*
[11] In re Estate of Green, 63 Ohio Misc. 44, 17 Ohio Op. 3d 338, 410 N.E.2d 812 (P. Ct. 1980). The allowance for support is discussed in Section 5.5 of this Chapter.
[12] *Id.*

real or personal property of the decedent not exceeding, with the decedent's interest in the mansion house and the land used with it, and the decedent's interest in the household goods (if the spouse chooses to purchase them), one-third of the appraised value of the gross estate.

Rights of Children

5.9 —Afterborn or Pretermitted Children

Section 2107.34 of the Revised Code states that if a child is born to or adopted by the testator after the testator has executed a Will[13] and no provision has been made for the child in the Will, then the pretermitted child may take an intestate share of the testator's property unless the testator's intention to disinherit the child is clear in the Will. The devises and legacies in the Will, except those to the surviving spouse, are abated proportionately to provide for the pretermitted child.[14]

5.10 —Disinherited Children

A testator may disinherit a child if the testator makes this intention clear in the Will.[15] While the intention to disinherit may be implied from the provisions of the Will,[16] the most prudent course is to state the testator's intention clearly:

> I give the residue of my estate, including all property not effectively transferred by the other provisions of my Will, to my daughter, *. I intentionally make no provision in my Will for my son, *.

5.11 —Adopted Children

A final decree of adoption creates the relationship of parent and child between the petitioner for adoption and the adopted child.

---

[13] R.C. § 2107.34 also applies to an heir designated under R.C. § 2105.15 after the will is executed and to a child or designated heir who was presumed dead but later is found alive.

[14] R.C. § 2107.34.

[15] 31 OHIO JUR. 3d *Decedents' Estates* § 275 (1981).

[16] Twitchell v. Alexander & Liggett, Inc., 115 Ohio App. 51, 20 Ohio Op. 2d 186, 184 N.E.2d 421 (1961); Spieldenner v. Spieldenner, 54 Ohio Op. 290, 122 N.E.2d 33 (P. Ct. 1954).

The adopted child is treated the same as a biological child for all purposes, including inheritance. Statutes, documents, and instruments apply to adopted children as well as to biological children, even where a statute, document, or instrument was effective before the adoption decree was final, unless adopted children are excluded expressly from the operation or effect of the statute or document.[17]

5.12 —Family Allowance

The surviving spouse and/or minor children of the decedent are entitled to an allowance for support, distributed in money or property from the estate's assets. This right is explained further in Section 5.5 of this Chapter.

5.13 Gifts to Charity

A bequest to a charity should clearly identify the charitable organization, including its location. If a bequest is made to a national or international organization, for example, the testator should state whether the bequest is made to the local office and, if so, should include the local address. When a bequest is made to a church, the church should be clearly identified because many churches have similar names. The following is an example of a charitable bequest:

> I give Fifty Thousand Dollars ($50,000.00) to The Planned Parenthood Association of Cincinnati, Inc., to be used as its governing board sees fit.

The testator should state whether the charitable gift must be used for a specific purpose. For example, a gift may be made to a university to be used for general educational purposes or a gift may be made specifically to establish a scholarship fund.

The testator may want to include a provision stating who will receive the bequest if the charity does not exist at the testator's death or if the charitable bequest is unenforceable for some reason.

Section 5731.17 of the Ohio Revised Code and I.R.C. § 2055 provide a deduction from the value of the gross estate for state and federal tax purposes for charitable bequests made to certain

---

[17] R.C. § 3107.15.

organizations. The attorney should consult these statutes and the federal regulations to determine the tax consequences of a charitable bequest made in a Will.

5.14 Conditional Bequests

A testator may attach a condition to a gift in a Will if the condition does not violate public policy or Ohio law.[18] If a condition is invalid, then it is inapplicable, but the gift itself does not fail.[19]

Numerous Ohio courts have examined the validity of certain conditions. For example, conditions in total restraint of marriage are void.[20] Some conditions on marriage, which amount to less than total restraint of marriage, have been upheld, however. A testator may make a provision for his or her surviving spouse conditioned on the surviving spouse not remarrying.[21] The testator may make a provision conditioned on the beneficiary marrying someone of a particular religious faith.[22] Conditioning a bequest on the recipient practicing a particular religion generally is considered a reasonable and valid condition.[23]

5.15 No Contest Provisions

The testator may include a no-contest or "in terrorem" provision in his or her Will. The no-contest provision generally provides that if a beneficiary contests the validity of a Will, then the beneficiary receives no benefit under the Will. The following is an example of a no-contest provision:

> If a beneficiary of my Will contests the validity of the Will, or any provision thereof, or joins in proceedings to contest the

[18] Case v. Hall, 52 Ohio St. 24, 38 N.E. 618 (1894).

[19] 32 OHIO JUR. 3d *Decedents' Estates* § 797 (1981).

[20] 32 OHIO JUR. 3d *Decedents' Estates* § 805 (1981) (citing Deckeback v. Stephany, 7 Ohio L. Rep. 113).

[21] Luigart v. Ripley, 19 Ohio St. 24 (1869); Saslow v. Saslow, 104 Ohio App. 157, 4 Ohio Op. 2d 230, 147 N.E.2d 262 (1957).

[22] Shapira v. Union Nat'l Bank, 39 Ohio Misc. 28, 66 Ohio Op. 2d 268, 315 N.E.2d 825 (C.P. 1974).

[23] *See* 32 OHIO JUR. 3d *Decedents' Estates* § 800 (1981). *But see* Moses v. Zook, 18 Ohio L. Abs. 373 (App. 1934) (holding that conditioning bequest on not marrying outside Protestant faith is against public policy).

validity of my Will, except as a defendant of the Will, regardless of whether the proceedings are instituted in good faith or with probable cause, then the contestant forfeits any right, title, and interest in my estate; all provisions of my Will for the benefit of the contestant are revoked; and any benefit that the contestant would have received shall be added to the residue of my estate and distributed accordingly, as if the contestant was never named or identified as a beneficiary under my Will.

While no-contest provisions generally are enforceable,[24] Ohio courts have questioned whether they should be enforced in all cases. For example, the appellate court in *Moskowitz v. Federman*[25] questioned the wisdom of allowing a no-contest provision to prevail when the grounds for the Will contest are fraud and undue influence, and the undue influence involved pressuring the testator to add a no-contest provision to the Will.

5.16 Ademption

An ademption takes place where something bequeathed does not exist at the testator's death or where the testator has made a lifetime gift as a substitute for the bequest, evidencing an intent to revoke the bequest.[26] "Ademption by extinction" occurs when property bequeathed or devised is transferred, lost, or destroyed.[27] A substantial change in the property may operate as an ademption.[28] For example, when property is sold and other property purchased with the proceeds of the sale, the purchased property is not a substitute and the devise or bequest fails.[29]

An "ademption by satisfaction" occurs when the testator makes a lifetime gift demonstrating his or her intention to revoke a testamentary gift.[30] The testator's intent is determinative; whether

[24] Irwin v. Jacques, 71 Ohio St. 395, 73 N.E. 683 (1905); Bradford v. Bradford, 19 Ohio St. 546 (1869).

[25] 72 Ohio App. 149, 163, 51 N.E.2d 48 (1943).

[26] 32 OHIO JUR. 3d *Decedents' Estates* § 897 (1981).

[27] Bool v. Bool, 165 Ohio St. 262, 135 N.E.2d 372 (1956); Gilbreath v. Alban, 10 Ohio 64 (1840).

[28] 32 OHIO JUR. 3d *Decedents' Estates* § 901 (1981).

[29] Bryan v. Bryan, 17 Ohio Op. 48, 31 Ohio L. Abs. 46 (P. Ct. 1939).

[30] Bool v. Bool, 165 Ohio St. 262, 135 N.E. 2d 372 (1956); Stichtenoth v. Toph, 10 Ohio Dec. Rep. 690 (1890).

a gift made by a testator is an ademption depends on the testator's intent at the time the gift is made.[31]

Some presumptions have developed with regard to the testator's intent. For example, if a parent makes a gift to a child in the parent's Will and the same parent subsequently makes a lifetime gift of the same character or purpose, the lifetime gift is presumed an ademption of the legacy, unless the testator expresses a contrary intention in his or her Will or elsewhere.[32]

5.17 Abatement

Abatement is a process whereby legacies and devises are reduced in amount when there are insufficient assets to pay the debts of the testator, the expenses of administering the estate, and the legacies in the testator's Will.[33] Abatement is relevant to drafting a simple Will because the testator may state in the Will his or her intentions regarding abatement; the testator's clearly expressed intentions will govern. The following is a sample provision clearly expressing the testator's intentions regarding abatement:

> If the assets of my estate are not sufficient to pay my bequests as well as my debts and expenses, then my Executor shall prorate the deficiency among the foregoing bequests so that the beneficiaries bear the loss equally.

The testator may provide that certain legacies will be abated before others or the testator may state the order in which the legacies will be abated. The testator may want to protect the surviving spouse and children by providing that the gifts to the other beneficiaries will be abated first.

If the testator does not state his or her intentions concerning abatement, then residual legacies and devises will be abated before general legacies and devises. General legacies and devises are abated before specific and specific are abated proportionately.[34]

---

[31] Bool v. Bool, 165 Ohio St. 262, 135 N.E.2d 372 (1956); Ellard v. Ferris, 91 Ohio St. 339, 110 N.E. 476 (1915).

[32] Ellard v. Ferris, 91 Ohio St. 339, 110 N.E. 476 (1915).

[33] *See* Gionfriddo v. Palatrone, 26 Ohio Op. 2d 158, 196 N.E.2d 162 (P. Ct. 1964).

[34] *Id.; see also* Harper v. Ohio Society for Crippled Children, Inc., 13 Ohio Op. 2d 160, 81 Ohio L. Abs. 91, 158 N.E.2d 747 (C.P. 1959).

Tax Apportionment

5.18 —General Rule

Ohio has enacted a statute governing the apportionment of estate taxes and generation-skipping transfer taxes.[35] The statute applies to federal estate taxes, federal generation-skipping taxes, Ohio estate taxes, and estate taxes imposed by any other jurisdiction on the transfer of property by the estate of a decedent domiciled in Ohio.[36]

The general rule provided by the apportionment statute is that, unless otherwise specified by the Will or other governing document, estate taxes are apportioned among all persons interested in the estate based on the value of each person's proportional interest.[37] The definition of the "estate" for purposes of apportionment is the same as the gross estate as defined for federal law,[38] for Ohio estate tax law,[39] or for estate tax purposes of any other jurisdiction imposing tax on a decedent domiciled in Ohio.[40]

The apportionment of Ohio and federal estate taxes may be governed by the decedent's intent if such an intent is clearly expressed in his or her Will[41] or trust agreement.[42] The testator's intent must be clear to shift the burden of the estate taxes.[43] To determine the intent of the testator, the language in the governing instrument is given its ordinary meaning.[44]

Federal law provides for the apportionment of the federal estate tax burden when it is imposed on the proceeds of life insurance,[45] property subject to a power of appointment,[46] and qualified ter-

---

[35] R.C. § 2113.85.

[36] R.C. §§ 2113.861, 2113.85(C).

[37] R.C. § 2113.86(A).

[38] I.R.C. §§ 2001 et seq.

[39] R.C. Chapter 5731.

[40] R.C. § 2113.85(B).

[41] McDougall v. Central Nat'l Bank, 157 Ohio St. 45, 47 Ohio Op. 60, 104 N.E.2d 441 (1952); Central Trust Co. v. Lamb, 74 Ohio App. 299, 29 Ohio Op. 457, 58 N.E.2d 785 (1944).

[42] *McDougall, supra,* n. 41.

[43] In re Estate of Carrington, 1 Ohio Op. 2d 72, 73 Ohio L. Abs. 381, 136 N.E.2d 182 (P. Ct. 1956); Oviatt v. Oviatt, 24 Ohio Misc. 98, 52 Ohio Op. 2d 325, 260 N.E.2d 136 (C.P. 1970).

[44] Wittenberg University v. Waterworth, 13 Ohio App. 3d 452, 13 O.B.R. 542, 469 N.E.2d 970 (1984).

[45] I.R.C. § 2206.

[46] I.R.C. § 2207.

minable interest property.[47] Except for these specified situations, state law governs the question of which property will bear the burden of the federal estate tax.[48]

5.19 —Exceptions to General Rule

There are three common exceptions to the general statutory rule that unless otherwise specified estate taxes are to be apportioned among persons interested in the estate based on the value of their proportional interests: specific bequests, property subject to an estate tax marital or charitable deduction, and property received as a spouse's elective share.

5.20 ——Specific Bequests

The tax apportioned to bequests that are not made under the residuary provisions of a Will or trust is reapportioned to the residue of the estate or trust. The tax that is reapportioned is charged in the same manner as a general administration expense. If a portion of the residue is allowed as a deduction, the tax will be reapportioned, to the extent possible, to the other part of the residue.[49] Often the exception happens more frequently than the general rule. The effect of this exception is that the Ohio estate taxes are first charged to the residue of the estate. Only when the taxes exceed the residue are they apportioned among the specific and nonresiduary bequests.[50]

5.21 ——Property Subject to Deductions

Where a transfer of property is subject to an estate tax marital or charitable deduction, then the estate tax is not apportioned against this interest in property, except to the extent that the interest is part of the residue against which the tax has been reapportioned.[51] Ohio law provides that the estate tax of Ohio or

[47] I.R.C. § 2207A.

[48] *McDougall, supra,* n. 41; *Wittenberg University, supra,* n. 44.

[49] R.C. § 2113.86(B).

[50] Boerstler v. Andrews, 30 Ohio App. 3d 63, 30 O.B.R. 118, 506 N.E.2d 279 (1986).

[51] R.C. § 2113.86(C)(1).

another jurisdiction shall not be reapportioned against an interest that is subject to a deduction for federal estate tax purposes. This provision applies to the extent that there is other property in the estate that is not subject to a deduction for federal estate tax purposes and against which the estate tax of Ohio or another jurisdiction can be apportioned.

5.22   ——Exemption of Spouse's Share

To the extent that there is other property in the estate against which the tax can be apportioned, the estate tax will not be apportioned against property received as a spouse's elective share[52] or as an intestate share.[53] Additionally, the statutory share of a spouse who elects to take against the Will is not altered by any provision in the Will.[54] Therefore, a spouse who elects to take against the Will cannot take advantage of any tax provision in the Will, but has the benefit of the apportionment statute, R.C. § 2113.86(D).

5.23   —Sample Apportionment Provisions

The following are examples of provisions regarding apportionment of taxes. The first directs the Executor to pay taxes from the residue of the estate:

> I direct my Executor to pay from the residue of my estate all estate, inheritance, and similar taxes and interest on taxes imposed because of my death, including taxes assessed with respect to insurance and other property passing outside of my Will.

The following provision directs the Executor to apportion the taxes among the beneficiaries:

> I direct my Executor to pay all estate, inheritance, and similar taxes and interest on taxes imposed because of my death. I further direct that the burden of such taxes shall be apportioned

[52] R.C. § 2106.01.
[53] R.C. §§ 2105.06, 2113.86(D).
[54] Weeks v. Vandeveer, 13 Ohio St. 2d 15, 42 Ohio Op. 2d 25, 233 N.E.2d 502 (1968).

among the beneficiaries of my taxable estate, including beneficiaries under my Will and beneficiaries of property passing outside my Will, but excluding the recipient(s) of my tangible personal property. My Executor shall take whatever actions are necessary to collect the taxes from such beneficiaries, including withholding from beneficiaries the amounts that they must contribute for the payment of taxes.

CHAPTER 6

Execution and Amendment of Will

6.1 Proper Execution

A person who is eighteen years old or older, of sound mind and memory, and not acting under restraint or duress may execute a Will.[1] A Will must be written, but may be handwritten or typed.[2] An oral Will with regard to the transfer of personal property is valid in Ohio only if made during "the last sickness" and put into writing and signed by two witnesses within ten days after the oral Will is made.[3]

A Will must be signed on the last page by the testator or by another person in the testator's presence and at the testator's direction.[4] Two or more witnesses, who saw the testator sign the instrument and/or heard the testator acknowledge it as the testator's Will, must sign the Will also.[5]

It is good practice to have the testator sign each page of the Will to make it clear that the testator intends each page to be part of his or her Will. It is likewise good practice to have both the testator and the witnesses sign on the last page of the Will to make it clear that the witnesses saw the testator sign the Will.

6.2 Amendment

A Will may be amended by a Codicil, which is an instrument executed with the same formalities as a Will and which modifies a

[1] R.C. § 2107.02.
[2] R.C. § 2107.03.
[3] R.C. § 2107.60.
[4] R.C. § 2107.03.
[5] *Id.*

provision or several provisions of a previously-executed Will. The Codicil should restate in its entirety each provision of the Will that the testator intends to modify. A Will may be amended by several Codicils; however, interpretation of the Will can become confusing and cumbersome when the Will consists of several different documents. After a Will has been amended several times, it is good practice to prepare a new Will rather than an additional Codicil. A Codicil form is included in Chapter 7 of this Handbook.

6.3 Revocation

A Will may be revoked by a subsequent Will or Codicil, by an act of the testator revoking the Will, or by operation of law. The testator may revoke a Will by tearing, canceling, obliterating, or destroying the Will with the intention of revoking it.[6] A testator may revoke a Will by directing another person in the testator's presence to tear up the testator's Will, or the testator may give an express written direction to another person to tear up the testator's Will.[7]

A Will or provisions of a Will may be revoked or amended by operation of law, such as by the divorce of the testator,[8] by the birth of the testator's child after the Will was executed and for whom there is no provision in the Will,[9] or by an alteration of the testator's interest in an item of property that the testator previously devised or bequeathed.[10]

Effect of Marriage/Divorce on Existing Wills

6.4 —Subsequent Marriage

Section 2107.37 of the Revised Code states that when an unmarried person executes a Will, the Will is not revoked when the testator subsequently marries.

[6] R.C. § 2107.33.
[7] *Id.*
[8] *Id.*
[9] R.C. § 2107.34.
[10] R.C. § 2107.36.

6.5 —Divorce

Section 2107.33 of the Revised Code provides that when a testator is divorced (or has the marriage dissolved or annulled), or separates from his or her spouse and enters a separation agreement intended to settle the prospective rights of the former spouses in each other's property, then the testator's disposition or appointment of property in the testator's Will to his or her former spouse, or to a trust over which the former spouse has powers, is revoked, unless the testator provides otherwise in his or her Will. The statute also states that if a Will grants a power of appointment to the former spouse or nominates the former spouse as executor, trustee, or guardian, then these provisions likewise are revoked, unless the testator provides otherwise in his or her Will.

Property passing because of revocation by R.C. § 2107.33 passes as if the former spouse predeceased the testator. Revoked provisions are considered revived by the testator's remarriage to the former spouse or upon termination of the separation agreement.

While a bequest to a former spouse is revoked by R.C § 2107.33, an alternate bequest dividing assets equally among the testator's children born of the marriage and the testator's stepchildren by reason of the marriage remains valid.[11]

Revised Code §§ 1339.63 and 1339.64 govern the effect of divorce upon jointly-held personal property and benefits arising under contracts. Revised Code § 1339.63 states that unless a beneficiary designation or divorce decree specifically provides otherwise, if a person designates a spouse as beneficiary and the parties subsequently divorce, the beneficiary designation is revoked as a result of the divorce and the former spouse is deemed to have predeceased the person who made the designation. Revised Code § 1339.63 applies to life insurance policies, annuities, payable on death accounts, individual retirement plans, employer death benefit plans, and other rights to death benefits arising under contract.

Revised Code § 1339.64 states that unless a divorce decree provides otherwise, if personal property is held for the joint lives of spouses and then to the survivor of them, the spouses' survivorship rights terminate when they obtain a divorce or dissolution of their marriage. Each former spouse is deemed the owner of an undivided

---

[11] Bowling v. Deaton, 31 Ohio App. 3d 17, 507 N.E.2d 1152 (1986).

interest in common, in proportion to the net contributions to the personal property.

APPENDIX A

Form Documents

FORM A   Estate Planning Questionnaire for Married Persons

I.   PERSONAL INFORMATION

	HUSBAND	WIFE
Name		
Home Address and Telephone Number		
Business Address and Telephone Number		
Date of Birth		
Place of Birth (Citizenship)		
Have you ever lived in any other state or foreign country? If so, where & when?		
Social Security Number		
Do you have a Will?		

II.   MARRIAGE INFORMATION

Date of Marriage		
Do you have financial obligations to a former spouse?		
Do you have an antenuptial agreement?		

III. FAMILY INFORMATION

	HUSBAND	WIFE
Names, addresses, and birthdates of children		
Names, addresses, and birthdates of grandchildren		
Persons other than children who are dependent upon you for support		

IV. ASSET INFORMATION

Description	Value	Form of Ownership and With Whom
Bank Accounts:		
Certificates of Deposit:		
Other Cash (money market funds, etc.):		

IV. ASSET INFORMATION

Description	Value	Form of Ownership and With Whom
Automobiles:		
Household Furnishings:		
Jewelry:		
Collections:		
Other Personal Property:		

Description	Value	Form of Ownership and With Whom
Securities (publicly traded):		
Closely-held Business (stock/ partnership); Subchapter S Stock:		
Real Estate (location, fair market value, amount of mortgage):		
Individual Retirement Accounts:		

Description	Value	Form of Ownership and With Whom
Employee Benefits & Government Benefits:		

Life Insurance Policies: (list additional policies on other side)

1. Company: _____

   Insured: _____

   Owner: _____

   Beneficiary: _____

   Face Value: _____

2. Company: _____

   Insured: _____

   Owner: _____

   Beneficiary: _____

   Face Value: _____

3. Company: _____

   Insured: _____

   Owner: _____

   Beneficiary: _____

   Face Value: _____

V. ESTATE PLANNING INFORMATION
(FOR MARRIED PERSONS)

1. How do you want your assets distributed upon your death?

2. Explain how you would like to provide for your spouse. If assets are to be distributed to your spouse, do you want them distributed outright or in trust?

3. Do any of your children have special needs?

4. If you and your spouse both die when your children are minors, should your children receive your property when they are 18 years old or should it be held until they are older? Should your children receive equal shares?

5. Do you want to make bequests to charitable organizations?

6. If neither your spouse nor your children survive you, who should receive your property?

7. Who would you like to serve as your fiduciaries? A fiduciary may be an individual or a bank.

   a. The **Executor** will manage your estate. He or she should be a resident of Ohio; however, out-of-state relatives (by blood or marriage) may serve.
      1.
      2.
      3.

b. The **Trustee** will manage your trust, if you decide to create one. The Trustee must invest and manage money, as well as maintain relationships with the beneficiaries and make decisions about distributions to the beneficiaries.
1.
2.
3.

c. A **Guardian** is responsible for the physical well-being, the estate, or both, of an incompetent or minor. Parents of young children frequently want to name relatives or friends to serve as guardians of their children if both parents die.
1.
2.
3.

8. Is minimizing income and estate taxes a high priority for you?

9. Would you like to make *lifetime* gifts to your children, other persons, or charity?

10. Would you like a Living Will, a Durable Power of Attorney for Health Care, or a general Durable Power of Attorney?

FORM B   Estate Planning Questionnaire For Single Persons

I.   PERSONAL INFORMATION

Name	
Home Address and Telephone Number	
Business Address and Telephone Number	
Date of Birth	
Place of Birth (Citizenship)	
Have you ever lived in any other state or foreign country? If so, where & when?	
Social Security Number	
Do you have a Will?	

II.   MARRIAGE INFORMATION

Do you have financial obligations to a former spouse?	

III. FAMILY INFORMATION

Names, addresses, and birthdates of children	
Names, addresses, and birthdates of grandchildren	
Persons other than children who are dependent upon you for support	

IV. ASSET INFORMATION

Description	Value	Form of Ownership and With Whom
Bank Accounts:		
Certificates of Deposit:		
Other Cash (money market funds, etc.):		

Description	Value	Form of Ownership and With Whom
Automobiles:		
Household Furnishings:		
Jewelry:		
Collections:		
Other Personal Property:		

Description	Value	Form of Ownership and With Whom
Securities (publicly traded):		
Closely-held Business (stock/ partnership); Subchapter S Stock:		
Real Estate (location, fair market value, amount of mortgage):		
Individual Retirement Accounts:		

Description	Value	Form of Ownership and With Whom
Employee Benefits & Government Benefits:		

Life Insurance Policies: (list additional policies on other side)

1. Company: _____

   Insured: _____

   Owner: _____

   Beneficiary: _____

   Face Value: _____

2. Company: _____

   Insured: _____

   Owner: _____

   Beneficiary: _____

   Face Value: _____

3. Company: _____

   Insured: _____

   Owner: _____

   Beneficiary: _____

   Face Value: _____

V. ESTATE PLANNING INFORMATION
(FOR SINGLE PERSONS)

1. How do you want your assets distributed upon your death?

2. If you have children, do any of your children have special needs?

3. If you die when your children are minors, should your children receive your property when they are 18 years old or should it be held until they are older? Should your children receive equal shares?

4. Do you want to make bequests to charitable organizations?

5. If none of your children survive you, who should receive your property?

6. Who would you like to serve as your fiduciaries? A fiduciary may be an individual or a bank.

   a. The **Executor** will manage your estate. He or she should be a resident of Ohio; however, out-of-state relatives (by blood or marriage) may serve.
      1.
      2.
      3.

   b. The **Trustee** will manage your trust, if you decide to create one. The Trustee must invest and manage money, as well as maintain relationships with the beneficiaries and make decisions about distributions to the beneficiaries.
      1.
      2.
      3.

   c. A **Guardian** is responsible for the physical well-being, the estate, or both, of an incompetent or minor. Parents of young children frequently want to name relatives or friends to serve as guardians of their children if both parents die.

     1.

     2.

     3.

7. Is minimizing income and estate taxes a high priority for you?

8. Would you like to make *lifetime* gifts to your children, other persons, or charity?

9. Would you like a Living Will, a Durable Power of Attorney for Health Care, or a general Durable Power of Attorney?

Form C   Simple Will

THE WILL
OF

_____

I, _____ , now a resident of _____ County, Ohio, make this my Will, and I revoke all prior Wills and Codicils made by me.

1. Tangible Personal Property

I give to my spouse, _____ , if my spouse survives me by thirty (30) days, my clothing, jewelry, household furniture, furnishings and equipment and all other items of tangible personal property owned by me at my death. If my spouse does not so survive me, I give my tangible personal property to my children who survive me by thirty (30) days, to be divided among them as they may agree. If my children cannot agree, then my Executor shall divide my tangible personal property among my children as nearly equally as practicable.

2. Residential Real Property

I give to my spouse, _____ , if my spouse survives me by thirty (30) days, any interest I may have in any residential real property at the time of my death, subject to any mortgage on the real property. If my spouse does not so survive me, this devise shall lapse.

_____

3. Residue

I give the residue of my estate to my spouse, _____ , if my spouse survives me by thirty (30) days. If my spouse does not so survive me, I give the residue of my estate to my then living lineal descendants, per stirpes.

4. Executor

I appoint one of the following persons, to be selected in the order named, as Executor of my Will. I direct that no bond be required of any of them for serving as Executor:

    1. _____

    2. _____

    3. _____

5. Debts and Taxes

My Executor shall pay out of the residue of my estate all of my just debts, including the expenses of my last illness, my funeral, and the administration of my estate.

My Executor shall pay out of the residue of my estate all estate taxes imposed because of my death, even though the taxes are assessed in whole or in part because of non-probate property. My Executor may exercise any elections available for federal or state tax law purposes and may claim deductions, even though an election or deduction may be more advantageous to one beneficiary than another, and shall not have to compensate any beneficiary who may be disadvantaged thereby. My Executor may file joint income tax returns with my spouse and may pay in full any taxes owed by my spouse and me, as shown on a joint income tax return, including taxes and interest owed because of an audit.

6. Executor's Powers

I give the Executor of my estate the authority to sell, rent, lease, mortgage, pledge, repair, improve, or convey any real or personal property upon the terms, including price, that my Executor decides are in the best interest of my estate; to invest and reinvest in whatever assets my Executor decides are appropriate; to make distributions in cash or in kind; to borrow money; to exercise (or not exercise) rights of ownership of securities, including the right to vote; to exercise (or not exercise) options to purchase securities; to employ agents, such as attorneys and investment advisers, to decide how much to pay them, and to pay them out of the residue of my estate; to disclaim any interest I may have in property; to compromise and settle claims in favor of or against my estate upon whatever terms my Executor decides are best; and the authority to take all other actions necessary for the proper administration and distribution of my estate.

7. Guardian

I request that the court of proper jurisdiction appoint as Guardian of the person and estate of any minor child of mine who survives me (if the child's other parent does not survive me) the first-named one of the following who can and will qualify to serve, and if the one qualifying ceases to serve for any reason, the next in the order named who can and will qualify to serve. I direct that no bond be required of any of them for serving as Guardian:

1. _____

2. _____

3. _____

IN WITNESS WHEREOF, I have signed this Will, consisting of _____ typewritten pages, on _____ , 19 ___ .

_____

*

This instrument was signed by the testator on the date above in our presence and declared by the testator to be the testator's Will. We have signed our names as witnesses, at the testator's request, in the testator's presence, and in the presence of each other.

_____ residing at _____

_____

_____ residing at _____

_____

Form D   Codicil to Will

[FIRST] CODICIL TO WILL
OF

_____

I, _____ , now a resident of _____ County, Ohio, do hereby make this the [First] Codicil to my Will dated _____ , 19 ___ .

I. I hereby amend Section _____ of my Will so that as amended it reads in its entirety as follows:

OR

I. I hereby delete Section _____ of my Will in its entirety, including all paragraphs thereof, and hereby substitute the following therefor:

In all other respects I hereby ratify and confirm my Will as originally written [and heretofore amended].

IN WITNESS WHEREOF, I have signed this my [First] Codicil to my Will [consisting, with this and the preceding pages, of (___) typewritten pages, each of which preceding pages I have also signed for greater security and better identification,] on _____ , 19 ___ .

_____

*

Use this for testator:

This instrument, bearing the signature of the Testator, *, was by him on the date last above written, signed and declared by him to be the [First] Codicil to his Will, in our presence, who at his request, and in his presence, and in the presence of each other, we believing him to be of sound and disposing mind and memory, have hereunto signed our names as witnesses.

_____ residing at _____

_____ residing at _____

_____

Use this for testatrix:

This instrument, bearing the signature of the Testatrix, *, was by her on the date last above written, signed and declared by her to be the [First] Codicil to her Will, in our presence, who at her request, and in her presence, and in the presence of each other, we believing her to be of sound and disposing mind and memory, have hereunto signed our names as witnesses.

_____ residing at _____

_____

_____ residing at _____

_____

APPENDIX B

Selected Statutory Provisions

§ 1339.63 Termination of marriage revokes designation of spouse as beneficiary of death benefits; immunity.

(A) As used in this section:

(1) "Beneficiary" means a beneficiary of a life insurance policy, an annuity, a payable on death account, an individual retirement plan, an employer death benefit plan, or another right to death benefits arising under a contract.

(2) "Employer death benefit plan" means any funded or unfunded plan or program, or any fund, that is established to provide the beneficiaries of an employee participating in the plan, program, or fund with benefits that may be payable upon the death of that employee.

(3) "Individual retirement plan" means an individual retirement account or individual retirement annuity as defined in section 408 of the "Internal Revenue Code of 1986," 100 Stat. 2085, 26 U.S.C. 408, as amended.

(B)(1) Unless the designation of beneficiary or the judgment or decree granting the divorce, dissolution of marriage, or annulment specifically provides otherwise, and subject to division (B)(2) of this section, if a spouse designates the other spouse as a beneficiary or if another person having the right to designate a beneficiary on behalf of the spouse designates the other spouse as a beneficiary, and if, after either type of designation, the spouse who made the designation or on whose behalf the designation was made, is divorced from the other spouse, obtains a dissolution of marriage, or has the marriage to the other spouse annulled, then the other spouse shall be deemed to have predeceased the spouse who made the designation or on whose behalf the designation was made, and the designation of the other spouse as a beneficiary is revoked as a result of the divorce, dissolution of marriage, or annulment.

(2) If the spouse who made the designation or on whose behalf the designation was made remarries the other spouse, then, unless the designation no longer can be made, the other spouse shall not be deemed to have predeceased the spouse who made the designation or on whose behalf the designation was made, and the designation of the other spouse as a beneficiary is not revoked because of the previous divorce, dissolution of marriage, or annulment.

(C) An agent, bank, broker, custodian, issuer, life insurance company, plan administrator, savings and loan association, transfer agent, trustee, or other person is not liable in damages or otherwise in a civil or criminal action or proceeding for distributing or disposing of property in reliance on and in accordance with a designation of beneficiary as described in division (B)(1) of this section, if both of the following apply:

(1) The distribution or disposition otherwise is proper;

(2) The agent, bank, broker, custodian, issuer, life insurance company, plan administrator, savings and loan association, transfer agent, trustee, or other person did not have any notice of the facts that resulted in the revocation of the beneficiary designation by operation of division (B)(1) of this section.

HISTORY: 143 v H 346. Eff 5-31-90.

§ 1339.64 Termination of survivorship rights of former spouse in personal property; immunity.

(A)(1) Unless the judgment or decree granting the divorce, dissolution of marriage, or annulment specifically provides otherwise, and subject to division (A)(2) of this section, if the title to any

personal property is held by two persons who are married to each other, if the title is so held for the joint lives of the spouses and then to the survivor of them, and if the marriage of the spouses subsequently is terminated by a judgment or decree granting a divorce, dissolution of marriage, or annulment, then the survivorship rights of the spouses terminate, and each spouse shall be deemed the owner of an undivided interest in common in the title to the personal property, that is in proportion to his net contributions to the personal property.

(2) If the spouses described in division (A)(1) of this section remarry each other and the title to the personal property continues to be held by them in accordance with that division, then the survivorship rights of the spouses are not terminated, and the spouses again hold title in the personal property for their joint lives and then to the survivor of them.

(B)(1) Unless the judgment or decree granting the divorce, dissolution of marriage, or annulment specifically provides otherwise, and subject to division (B)(2) of this section, if the title to any personal property is held by more than two persons and at least two of the persons are married to each other, if the title is so held for the joint lives of the titleholders and then to the survivor or survivors of them, and if the marriage of any of the titleholders who are married to each other subsequently is terminated by a judgment or decree granting a divorce, dissolution of marriage, or annulment, then the survivorship rights of the titleholders who were married to each other terminate, the survivorship rights of the other titleholders are not affected, and each of the titleholders who were married to each other shall be deemed to be the owner of an undivided interest in common in the personal property, that is in proportion to his net contributions to the personal property.

(2) If the titleholders who were married to each other as described in division (B)(1) of this section remarry each other, and if the title to the personal

property continues to be held by them, and the other titleholders whose survivorship rights continued unaffected, in accordance with that division, then the survivorship rights of the remarried titleholders are not terminated, and the remarried and other titleholders again hold title in the personal property for their joint lives and then to the survivor or survivors of them.

(C) An agent, bank, broker, custodian, issuer, life insurance company, plan administrator, savings and loan association, transfer agent, trustee, or other person is not liable in damages or otherwise in a civil or criminal action or proceeding for distributing or disposing of personal property in reliance on and in accordance with a registration in the form of a joint ownership for life, with rights of survivorship, as described in division (A)(1) or (B)(1) of this section, if both of the following apply:

(1) The distribution or disposition otherwise is proper;

(2) The agent, bank, broker, custodian, issuer, life insurance company, plan administrator, savings and loan association, transfer agent, trustee, or other person did not have any notice of the facts that resulted in the termination of the rights of survivorship by operation of division (A)(1) or (B)(1) of this section.

HISTORY: 143 v H 346. Eff 5-31-90.

§ 1340.04 Effect of date of receipt on right to income.

(A) An income beneficiary is entitled to income from the date specified in the trust instrument, or, if none is specified, from the date an asset becomes subject to the trust.

(B) In all other cases, any receipt from an income producing asset is income even though the receipt was earned or accrued in whole or in part before the date when the asset became subject to the trust.

(C) On termination of an income interest, the income beneficiary whose interest is terminated, or his estate, is entitled to:

(1) Income undistributed on the date of termination;

(2) Income due but not paid to the trustee on the date of termination;

(3) Income in the form of periodic payments, other than corporate distributions to stockholders, including rent, interest, or annuities, not due on the date of termination, accrued from day to day.

(D) Corporate distributions to stockholders shall be treated as due on the day fixed by the corporation for determination of stockholders of record entitled to distribution, or, if no date is fixed, on the date of declaration of the distribution by the corporation. Distributions to corporate trustees may be treated as due on the ex-dividend date in lieu of the record date, if such corporate trustee consistently uses this date with respect to all of its trusts under administration.

HISTORY: 142 v S 146. Eff 10-20-87.

§ 2105.06 Statute of descent and distribution.

When a person dies intestate having title or right to any personal property, or to any real estate or inheritance, in this state, the personal property shall be distributed, and the real estate or inheritance shall descend and pass in parcenary, except as otherwise provided by law, in the following course:

(A) If there is no surviving spouse, to the children of the intestate or their lineal descendants, per stirpes;

(B) If there is a spouse and one child or its lineal descendants surviving, the first sixty thousand dollars if the spouse is the natural or adoptive parent of the child, or the first twenty thousand dollars if the spouse is not the natural or adoptive parent of the child, plus one-half of the balance of the intestate estate to the spouse and the remainder to the child or his lineal descendants, per stirpes;

(C) If there is a spouse and more than one child or their lineal descendants surviving, the first sixty thousand dollars if the spouse is the natural or adoptive parent of one of the children, or the first twenty thousand dollars if the spouse is the natural or adoptive parent of none of the children, plus one-third of the balance of the intestate estate to the spouse and the remainder to the children equally, or to the lineal descendants of any deceased child, per stirpes;

(D) If there are no children or their lineal descendants, then the whole to the surviving spouse;

(E) If there is no spouse and no children or their lineal descendants, to the parents of the intestate equally, or to the surviving parent;

(F) If there is no spouse, no children or their lineal descendants, and no parent surviving, to the brothers and sisters, whether of the whole or of the half blood of the intestate, or their lineal descendants, per stirpes;

(G) If there are no brothers or sisters or their lineal descendants, one-half to the paternal grandparents of the intestate equally, or to the survivor of them, and one-half to the maternal grandparents of the intestate equally, or to the survivor of them;

(H) If there is no paternal grandparent or no maternal grandparent, one-half to the lineal descendants of the deceased grandparents, per stirpes; if there are no such lineal descendants, then to the surviving grandparents or their lineal descendants, per stirpes; if there are no surviving grandparents or their lineal descendants, then to the next of kin of the intestate, provided there shall be no representation among such next of kin;

(I) If there are no next of kin, to stepchildren or their lineal descendants, per stirpes;

(J) If there are no stepchildren or their lineal descendants, escheat to the state.

HISTORY: GC § 10503-4; 114 v 320(339); 116 v 385; Bureau of Code Revision, 10-1-53; 128 v 155 (Eff 11-9-59); 136 v S 145 (Eff 1-1-76); 136 v S 466 (Eff 5-26-76); 141 v S 248. Eff 12-17-86.

[§ 2105.06.1] § 2105.061
Passing of real property subject to monetary charge of surviving spouse.

Except any real property that a surviving spouse elects to receive under section 2106.10 of the Revised Code, the title to real property in an intestate estate shall descend and pass in parcenary to those persons entitled to it under division (B) or (C) of section 2105.06 of the Revised Code, subject to the monetary charge of the surviving spouse. The administrator or executor shall file an application for a certificate of transfer as provided in section 2113.61 of the Revised Code, which shall include a statement of the amount of money that remains due and payable to the surviving spouse as found by the probate court. The certificate of transfer ordered by the probate court shall recite that the title to the real property described in the certificate is subject to the monetary charge in favor of the surviving spouse, and shall recite the value in dollars of the charge on the title to the real property included in the certificate.

HISTORY: 143 v H 346. Eff 5-31-90.

§ 2105.21 Presumption of order of death.

When there is no evidence of the order in which the death of two or more persons occurred, no one of such persons shall be presumed to have died first and the estate of each shall pass and descend as though he had survived the others. When the surviving spouse or other heir at law, legatee or devisee dies within thirty days after the death of the decedent, the estate of such first decedent shall pass and descend as though he had survived such surviving spouse, or other heir at law, legatee or devisee. A beneficiary of a testamentary trust shall not be deemed to be a legatee or devisee within the meaning of this section. This section shall prevail over the right of election of a surviving spouse.

This section shall not apply in the

case of wills wherein provision has been made for distribution of property different from the provisions of this section. In such case such provision of the will shall not prevail over the right of election of a surviving spouse.

HISTORY: GC § 10503-18; 114 v 320(343); Bureau of Code Revision, 10-1-53; 125 v 903(963); 125 v 411. Eff 10-16-53.

§ 2106.01 Election by surviving spouse.

(A) After the probate of a will and the filing of the inventory and the appraisement, the probate court shall issue a citation to the surviving spouse, if any is living at the time of the issuance of the citation, to elect whether to take under the will or under section 2105.06 of the Revised Code.

(B) If the surviving spouse elects to take under section 2105.06 of the Revised Code and if the value of the property that the surviving spouse is entitled to receive is equal to or greater than the value of the decedent's interest in the mansion house as determined under section 2106.10 of the Revised Code, the surviving spouse also is entitled to make an election pursuant to division (A) of section 2106.10 of the Revised Code.

(C) If the surviving spouse elects to take under section 2105.06 of the Revised Code, the surviving spouse shall take not to exceed one-half of the net estate, unless two or more of the decedent's children or their lineal descendants survive, in which case the surviving spouse shall take not to exceed one-third of the net estate.

For purposes of this division, the net estate shall be determined before payment of federal estate tax, estate taxes under Chapter 5731. of the Revised Code, or any other tax that is subject to apportionment under section 2113.86 or 2113.861 [2113.86.1] of the Revised Code.

(D) Unless the will expressly provides that in case of an election under division (A) of this section there shall be no acceleration of remainder or other interests

bequeathed or devised by the will, the balance of the net estate shall be disposed of as though the surviving spouse had predeceased the testator. If there is a disposition by a will to an inter vivos trust that was created by the testator, if under the terms of the trust the surviving spouse is entitled to any interest in the trust or is granted any power or nomination with respect to the trust, and if the surviving spouse makes an election to take under section 2105.06 of the Revised Code, then, unless the trust instrument provides otherwise, the surviving spouse is deemed for purposes of the trust to have predeceased the testator, and there shall be an acceleration of remainder or other interests in all property bequeathed or devised to the trust by the will, in all property held by the trustee at the time of the death of the decedent, and in all property that comes into the hands of the trustee by reason of the death of the decedent.

(E) The election of a surviving spouse to take under a will or under section 2105.06 of the Revised Code may be made at any time after the death of the decedent, but shall be made not later than one month from the service of the citation to elect. On a motion filed before the expiration of the one-month period, and for good cause shown, the court may allow further time for the making of the election. If no action is taken by the surviving spouse before the expiration of the one-month period, it is conclusively presumed that the surviving spouse elects to take under the will. The election shall be entered on the journal of the court.

When proceedings for advice or to contest the validity of a will are begun within the time allowed by this division for making the election, the election may be made within three months after the final disposition of the proceedings, if the will is not set aside.

(F) When a surviving spouse succeeds to the entire estate of the testator, having been named the sole devisee and legatee, it shall be presumed that the spouse elects to take under the will of the testator. No citation shall be issued to the surviving spouse as provided in division (A) of this section, and no election shall be required, unless the surviving spouse manifests a contrary intention.

HISTORY: GC §§ 10504-55, 10504-58; 114 v 320(357); 116 v 385; 119 v 394; Bureau of Code Revision, RC § 2107.39, 10-1-53; 125 v 411 (Eff 10-16-53); 133 v S 185 (Eff 1-1-71); 135 v H 374 (Eff 10-31-73); 136 v S 145 (Eff 1-1-76); 138 v S 317 (Eff 3-23-81); 141 v H 139 (Eff 7-24-86); 141 v S 248 (Eff 12-17-86); 142 v S 228 (Eff 3-22-89); RC § 2106.01, 143 v H 346. Eff 5-31-90.

§ 2106.02 Citation to make the election.

(A) The citation to make the election referred to in section 2106.01 of the Revised Code shall be sent to the surviving spouse by certified mail. Notice that the citation has been issued by the court shall be given to the administrator or executor of the estate of the deceased spouse.

(B) The citation shall be accompanied by a general description of the effect of the election and the general rights of the surviving spouse. The description shall include a specific reference to the procedures available to the surviving spouse under section 2106.03 of the Revised Code and to the presumption that arises if the surviving spouse does not make the election in accordance with division (E) of section 2106.01 of the Revised Code. The description of the effect of the election and of the rights of the surviving spouse need not relate to the nature of any particular estate.

(C) A surviving spouse electing to take under the will may manifest the election in writing within the times described in division (E) of section 2106.01 of the Revised Code.

HISTORY: RC § 2107.39.1, 136 v S 145 (Eff 1-1-76); 136 v S 466 (Eff 5-26-76); RC § 2106.02, 143 v H 346. Eff 5-31-90.

§ 2106.03 Complaint; construction of will.

Within the times described in division (E) of section 2106.01 of the Revised Code for making an election, the surviving spouse may file a complaint in the probate court making all persons interested in the will defendants, that requests a construction of the will in favor of the surviving spouse and for the court to render a judgment to that effect.

HISTORY: GC § 10504-57; 114 v 320(357); 118 v 78; Bureau of Code Revision, RC § 2107.40, 10-1-53; 136 v S 145 (Eff 1-1-76); RC § 2106.03, 143 v H 346. Eff 5-31-90.

§ 2106.04 Failure to make election; presumption.

If the surviving spouse dies before probate of the will, or, having survived the probate, thereafter either fails to make the election provided by section 2106.01 of the Revised Code or dies without having made an election within the times described in division (E) of that section, the surviving spouse shall be conclusively presumed to have elected to take under the will, and the surviving spouse and the heirs, devisees, and legatees of the surviving spouse, and those claiming through or under them, shall be bound by the conclusive presumption, and persons may deal with the property of the decedent accordingly; provided that, if applicable, the provisions of section 2105.21 of the Revised Code shall prevail over the provisions relating to the right of election of a surviving spouse.

HISTORY: GC § 10504-60; 114 v 320(357); 116 v 385; 122 v 498; Bureau of Code Revision, RC § 2107.41, 10-1-53; 125 v 411 (Eff 10-16-53); RC § 2106.04, 143 v H 346. Eff 5-31-90.

§ 2106.05 Election to take under the will; effect.

If a surviving spouse elects to take under the will, the surviving spouse shall be barred of all right to an intestate share of the property passing under the will and shall take under the will alone, unless it plainly appears from the will that the provision for the surviving spouse was intended to be in addition to an intestate share. An election to take under the will does not bar the right of the surviving spouse to an intestate share of that portion of the estate as to which the decedent dies intestate. Unless the will expressly otherwise directs, an election to take under the will does not bar the right of the surviving spouse to remain in the mansion house, and does not bar the right of the surviving spouse to receive the allowance for the support provided by section 2106.13 of the Revised Code.

HISTORY: GC § 10504-61; 114 v 320(357); 116 v 385; 119 v 394; Bureau of Code Revision, RC § 2107.42, 10-1-53; 136 v S 145 (Eff 1-1-76); RC § 2106.05, 143 v H 346. Eff 5-31-90.

§ 2106.06 Election made in person.

The election of a surviving spouse to take under section 2105.06 of the Revised Code and thereby refusing to take under the will shall be made in person before the probate judge, or a deputy clerk who has been appointed to act as a referee, except as provided in sections 2106.07 and 2106.08 of the Revised Code.

When the election is made in person before the judge or referee, the judge or referee shall explain the will, the rights under the will, and the rights, by law, in the event of a refusal to take under the will.

HISTORY: GC §§ 10504-56, 10504-59; 114 v 320(357); 122 v 498; Bureau of Code Revision, RC § 2107.43, 10-1-53; 125 v 411 (Eff 10-16-53); 136 v S 145 (Eff 1-1-76); 136 v S 466 (Eff 5-26-76); RC § 2106.06, 143 v H 346. Eff 5-31-90.

§ 2106.07 Commission issued to take election of spouse.

Upon the filing of an application on behalf of a surviving spouse, the probate court may issue a commission, with a copy of the will annexed, directed to any suitable person, to take the election of the surviving spouse as described in section 2106.01 of the Revised Code. In the commission, the court shall direct the suitable person to explain the rights of the surviving spouse under the will and

under Chapter 2105. of the Revised Code.

HISTORY: GC § 10504-62; 114 v 320(358); 122 v 498; Bureau of Code Revision, RC § 2107.44, 10-1-53; RC § 2106.07, 143 v H 346. Eff 5-31-90.

§ 2106.08 Election made by one under legal disability.

If, because of a legal disability, a surviving spouse is unable to make an election as provided by section 2106.01 of the Revised Code, as soon as the facts come to the knowledge of the probate court, the probate court shall appoint some suitable person to ascertain the value of the provision made for the surviving spouse by the testator, the value of the rights of the surviving spouse in the estate of the testator under Chapter 2105. of the Revised Code, and the adequate support needs of the surviving spouse after taking into consideration the other available resources and the age, probable life expectancy, physical and mental condition, and present and reasonably anticipated future needs of the surviving spouse. The appointment by the court shall be made at any time within the times described in division (E) of section 2106.01 of the Revised Code for making an election under that section.

When the person so appointed returns the report of his investigation, the court may elect for the surviving spouse to take under section 2105.06 of the Revised Code only if it finds, after taking into consideration the other available resources and the age, probable life expectancy, physical and mental condition, and present and reasonably anticipated future needs of the surviving spouse, that the election to take under section 2105.06 of the Revised Code is necessary to provide adequate support for the surviving spouse during his life expectancy.

After making its determination under this section, the court shall record upon its journal the election made for the surviving spouse. The election, when so entered, shall have the same effect as an election made by one not under legal disability.

HISTORY: GC §§ 10504-63, 10504-64; 114 v 320(358); Bureau of Code Revision, RC § 2107.45, 10-1-53; 125 v 903(963) (Eff 10-1-53); 141 v S 248 (Eff 12-17-86); RC § 2106.08, 143 v H 346. Eff 5-31-90.

§ 2106.11 Payment of specific monetary share to surviving spouse; charge on realty.

Subject to the right of the surviving spouse to elect to receive the decedent's interest in the mansion house pursuant to section 2106.10 of the Revised Code, the specific monetary share payable to a surviving spouse under division (B) or (C) of section 2105.06 of the Revised Code shall be paid out of the tangible and intangible personal property in the intestate estate to the extent that the personal property is available for distribution. The personal property distributed to the surviving spouse, other than cash, shall be valued at the appraised value.

Before tangible and intangible personal property is transferred to the surviving spouse in payment or part payment of the specific monetary share, the administrator or executor shall file an application that includes an inventory of the personal property intended to be distributed in kind to the surviving spouse, together with a statement of the appraised value of each item of personal property included. The court shall examine the application and make a finding of the amount of personal property to be distributed to the surviving spouse, and shall order that the personal property be distributed to the surviving spouse. The court concurrently shall make a finding of the amount of money that remains due and payable to the surviving spouse in satisfaction of the specific monetary share to which the surviving spouse is entitled under division (B) or (C) of section 2105.06 of the Revised Code. Any amount that remains due and payable shall be a charge on the title to any real property in the estate but the charge does not bear interest. This charge may be conveyed or released in the same manner as any other interest in real estate and may be enforced by foreclosure or any other appropriate remedy.

HISTORY: RC § 2105.06.3, 136 v S 466 (Eff 5-26-76); 141 v S 248 (Eff 12-17-86); RC § 2106.11, 143 v H 346. Eff 5-31-90.

§ 2106.13 Allowance for support.

(A) If a person dies leaving a surviving spouse and no minor children, leaving a surviving spouse and minor children, or leaving minor children and no surviving spouse, the surviving spouse, minor children, or both shall be entitled to receive, subject to division (B) of this section, in money or property the sum of twenty-five thousand dollars as an allowance for support. The money or property set off as an allowance shall be considered estate assets.

(B) The probate court shall order the distribution of the allowance for support described in division (A) of this section as follows:

(1) If the person died leaving a surviving spouse and no minor children, one hundred per cent to the surviving spouse;

(2) If the person died leaving a surviving spouse and minor children, and if all of the minor children are the children of the surviving spouse, one hundred per cent to the surviving spouse;

(3) If the person died leaving a surviving spouse and minor children, and if not all of the minor children are children of the surviving spouse, in equitable shares, as fixed by the probate court in accordance with this division, to the surviving spouse and the minor children who are not the children of the surviving spouse. In determining equitable shares under this division, the probate court shall do all of the following:

(a) Consider the respective needs of the surviving spouse, the minor children who are children of the surviving spouse, and the minor children who are not children of the surviving spouse;

(b) Allocate to the surviving spouse, the share that is equitable in light of the needs of the surviving spouse and the minor children who are children of the surviving spouse;

(c) Allocate to the minor children who are not children of the surviving spouse, the share that is equitable in light of the needs of those minor children.

(4) If the person died leaving minor children and no surviving spouse, in equitable shares, as fixed by the probate court in accordance with this division, to the minor children. In determining equitable shares under this division, the probate court shall consider the respective needs of the minor children and allocate to each minor child the share that is equitable in light of his needs.

HISTORY: RC § 2117.20, 136 v S 145 (Eff 1-1-76); RC § 2106.13, 143 v H 346. Eff 5-31-90.

§ 2106.15 Mansion house.

A surviving spouse may remain in the mansion house free of charge for one year, except that such real property may be sold within that time for the payment of debts of the decedent. If the real property is so sold, the surviving spouse shall be compensated from the estate to the extent of the fair rental value for the unexpired term, such compensation to have the same priority in payment of debts of estates as the allowance for support made to the surviving spouse, minor children, or surviving spouse and minor children of the decedent under section 2106.13 of the Revised Code.

HISTORY: GC § 10509-79; 114 v 320(418); Bureau of Code Revision, RC § 2117.24, 10-1-53; 136 v S 466 (Eff 5-26-76); RC § 2106.15, 143 v H 346. Eff 5-31-90.

§ 2106.16 Purchase of property by surviving spouse.

A surviving spouse, even though acting as executor or administrator, may purchase the following property, if left by the decedent, and if not specifically devised or bequeathed:

(A) The decedent's interest in the mansion house, including the decedent's title in the parcel of land on which such house is situated and lots or farm land adjacent to the house and used in conjunction with it as the home of the decedent, and the decedent's title in the household goods contained in the house, at the appraised value as fixed by the appraisers;

(B) Any other real or personal property of the decedent not exceeding, with the decedent's interest in the mansion house and the decedent's title in the land used in conjunction with it, and the decedent's title in the household goods the spouse elects to purchase, one-third of the gross appraised value of the estate, at the appraised value as fixed by the appraisers.

A spouse desiring to exercise this right of purchase with respect to personal property shall file in the probate court an application setting forth an accurate description of the personal property, and the election of the spouse to purchase it at the appraised value. No notice is required for the court to hear the application, insofar as it appertains to household goods contained in the mansion house. If the application includes other personal property, the court shall cause a notice of the time and place of the hearing of the application with respect to such other personal property to be given to the executor or administrator, the heirs or beneficiaries interested in the estate, and to such other interested persons as the court determines.

A spouse desiring to exercise this right of purchase with respect to an interest in real property shall file in the court a petition containing an accurate description of the real property, and naming as parties defendant the executor or administrator, the persons to whom the real property passes by inheritance or residuary devise, and all mortgagees and other lienholders whose claims affect the real property or any part of it. Spouses of parties defendant need not be made parties defendant. The petition shall set forth the election of the surviving spouse to purchase the interest in real property at the appraised value, and shall contain a prayer accordingly. A summons upon that petition shall be issued and served on the defendants, in the same manner as provided for service of summons in actions to sell real property to pay debts.

No hearing on the application or petition shall be held until the inventory is approved. On the hearing of the application or petition, the finding of the court shall be in favor of the surviving spouse, unless it appears that the appraisement was made as a result of collusion or fraud, or that it is so manifestly inadequate that a sale at that price would unconscionably prejudice the rights of the parties in interest or creditors. The action of the court shall not be held to prejudice the rights of lienholders.

Upon a finding in favor of the surviving spouse, the court shall make an entry fixing the terms of payment to the executor or administrator for the property, having regard for the rights of creditors of the estate, and ordering the executor or administrator, or a commissioner who may be appointed and authorized for the purpose, to transfer and convey the property to the spouse upon compliance with the terms fixed by the court. If the court, having regard for the amount of property to be purchased, its appraised value, and the distribution to be made of the proceeds arising from the sale, finds that the original bond given by the executor or administrator is sufficient, the court may dispense with the giving of additional bonds. If the court finds that the original bond is insufficient, as a condition to transfer and conveyance, the court shall require the executor or administrator to execute an additional bond in an amount as the court may fix, with proper surety, conditioned and payable as provided in section 2127.27 of the Revised Code. This section does not prevent the court from ordering transfer and conveyance without bond in cases where the will of a testator provides that the executor need not give bond. The executor or administrator, or a commissioner, then shall execute and deliver to the surviving spouse a proper bill of sale or deed, as the case may be, for the property, and make a return to the court.

The death of the surviving spouse prior to the filing of the court's entry fixing the terms of payment for property elected to be purchased shall nullify the election. The real or personal property then shall be free of the right granted in this section.

The application or petition provided for in this section shall not be filed prior to filing the inventory, nor later than one month after the approval of the inventory required by section 2115.02 of the Revised Code. Failure to file an application or petition within that time nullifies the election with respect to the property required to be included, and the real or personal property then shall be free of the right granted in this section.

HISTORY: GC § 10509-89; 114 v 320(420); 116 v 385(396); 119 v 394(406); 123 v 460; Bureau of Code Revision, RC § 2113.38, 10-1-53; 125 v 903(975) (Eff 10-1-53); 132 v S 398 (Eff 4-29-68); 136 v S 145 (Eff 1-1-76); 141 v S 248 (Eff 12-17-86); RC § 2106.16, 143 v H 346. Eff 5-31-90.

§ 2106.18 Transfer of automobile title.

(A) Upon the death of a married resident who owned at least one automobile at the time of death, the interest of the deceased spouse in one automobile that is not otherwise specifically disposed of by testamentary disposition and that is selected by the surviving spouse immediately shall pass to the surviving spouse upon transfer of title to the automobile in accordance with section 4505.10 of the Revised Code. The automobile shall not be considered an estate asset and shall not be included and stated in the estate inventory.

(B) The executor or administrator, with the approval of the probate court, may transfer title to an automobile owned by the decedent:

(1) To the surviving spouse, when the automobile is purchased by the surviving spouse pursuant to section 2106.16 of the Revised Code;

(2) To a distributee;

(3) To a purchaser.

(C) The executor or administrator may transfer title to an automobile owned by the decedent without the approval of the probate court:

(1) To a legatee entitled to the automobile under the terms of the will;

(2) To a distributee if the distribution of the automobile is made without court order pursuant to section 2113.55 of the Revised Code;

(3) To a purchaser if the sale of the automobile is made pursuant to section 2113.39 of the Revised Code.

(D) As used in division (A) of this section, "automobile" includes a truck, if the deceased spouse did not own an automobile and if the truck was used as a method of conveyance by the deceased spouse or his family when the deceased spouse was alive.

HISTORY: RC § 2113.53.2, 133 v S 185 (Eff 1-1-71); 136 v S 145 (Eff 1-1-76); 136 v S 466 (Eff 5-26-76); 137 v S 277 (Eff 1-13-78); 139 v H 620 (Eff 9-9-82); 140 v S 260 (Eff 9-20-84); RC § 2106.18, 143 v H 346. Eff 5-31-90.

§ 2106.20 Reimbursement for funeral expenses.

A surviving spouse is entitled to a reimbursement from the estate of the deceased spouse for funeral expenses, if paid by the surviving spouse, to the extent that the rights of other creditors of the estate will not be prejudiced by the reimbursement.

HISTORY: GC § 10509-125; 114 v 320(429); Bureau of Code Revision, RC § 2117.26, 10-1-53; 129 v 1265 (Eff 8-4-61); RC § 2106.20, 143 v H 346. Eff 5-31-90.

§ 2106.22 Action to set aside antenuptial or separation agreement.

Any antenuptial or separation agreement to which a decedent was a party is valid unless an action to set it aside is commenced within four months after the appointment of the executor or administrator of the estate of the decedent, or unless, within the four-month period, the validity of the agreement otherwise is attacked.

HISTORY: GC § 10512-3; 114 v 320(469); Bureau of Code Revision, RC § 2131.03, 10-1-53; RC § 2106.22, 143 v H 346. Eff 5-31-90.

§ 2106.24 Additional rights of surviving spouse.

In addition to the rights provided in this chapter, a surviving spouse of a decedent who died testate or intestate is entitled to any other rights prescribed in other chapters of the Revised Code, including, but not limited to, any dower rights under Chapters 2103. and 5305. of the Revised Code.

HISTORY: 143 v H 346. Eff 5-31-90.

§ 2107.01 Definition.

In Chapters 2101. to 2131., inclusive, of the Revised Code, "will" includes codicils and lost, spoliated, or destroyed wills.

HISTORY: GC § 10504-1; 114 v 320(346); Bureau of Code Revision. Eff 10-1-53.

§ 2107.02 Who may make will.

A person of the age of eighteen years, or over, [of] sound mind and memory, and not under restraint[,] may make a will.

HISTORY: GC § 10504-2; 114 v 320(346); Bureau of Code Revision, 10-1-53; 131 v 617. Eff 8-10-65.

§ 2107.03 Method of making will.

Except oral wills, every last will and testament shall be in writing, but may be handwritten or typewritten. Such will shall be signed at the end by the party making it, or by some other person in such party's presence and at his express direction, and be attested and subscribed in the presence of such party, by two or more competent witnesses, who saw the testator subscribe, or heard him acknowledge his signature.

HISTORY: GC § 10504-3; 114 v 320(346); Bureau of Code Revision. Eff 10-1-53.

§ 2107.04　Agreement to make a will.

No agreement to make a will or to make a devise or bequest by will shall be enforceable unless it is in writing. Such agreement must be signed by the maker or by some other person at such maker's express direction. If signed by a person other than such maker, the instrument must be subscribed by two or more competent witnesses who heard such maker acknowledge that it was signed at his direction.

HISTORY: GC § 10504-3a; 116 v 385(404), § 2; Bureau of Code Revision. Eff 10-1-53.

§ 2107.05　Incorporation by reference.

An existing document, book, record, or memorandum may be incorporated in a will by reference, if referred to as being in existence at the time the will is executed. Such document, book, record, or memorandum shall be deposited in the probate court when the will is probated or within thirty days thereafter, unless the court grants an extension of time for good cause shown. A copy may be substituted for the original document, book, record, or memorandum if such copy is certified to be correct by a person authorized to take acknowledgments on deeds.

HISTORY: GC § 10504-4; 114 v 320(346); Bureau of Code Revision. Eff 10-1-53.

§ 2107.33　Revocation of will.

(A) A will shall be revoked by the testator by tearing, canceling, obliterating, or destroying it with the intention of revoking it, or by some person in the testator's presence, or by the testator's express written direction, or by some other written will or codicil, executed as prescribed by sections 2107.01 to 2107.62 of the Revised Code, or by some other writing that is signed, attested, and subscribed in the manner provided by those sections. A will that has been declared valid and is in the possession of a probate judge may also be revoked according to division (C) of section 2107.084 [2107.08.4] of the Revised Code.

(B) If a testator removes a will that has been declared valid and is in the possession of a probate judge pursuant to section 2107.084 [2107.08.4] of the Revised Code from the possession of the judge, the declaration of validity that was rendered no longer has any effect.

(C) If after executing a will, a testator is divorced, obtains a dissolution of marriage, has his marriage annulled, or, upon actual separation from his spouse, enters into a separation agreement pursuant to which the parties intend to fully and finally settle their prospective property rights in the property of the other, whether by expected inheritance or otherwise, any disposition or appointment of property made by the will to the former spouse or to a trust with powers created by or available to the former spouse, any provision in the will conferring a general or special power of appointment on the former spouse, and any nomination in the will of the former spouse as executor, trustee, or guardian, shall be revoked unless the will expressly provides otherwise.

(D) Property prevented from passing to a former spouse or to a trust with powers created by or available to the former spouse because of revocation by this section shall pass as if the former spouse failed to survive the decedent, and other provisions conferring some power or office on the former spouse shall be interpreted as if the spouse failed to survive the decedent. If provisions are revoked solely by this section, they shall be deemed to be revived by the testator's remarriage with the former spouse or upon the termination of a separation agreement executed by them.

(E) A bond, agreement, or covenant made by a testator, for a valuable consideration, to convey property previously devised or bequeathed in a will, does not revoke the devise or bequest. The property passes by the devise or bequest, subject to the remedies on the bond, agreement, or covenant, for a specific performance or otherwise, against the devisees or legatees, that might be had by law against the heirs of the testator, or his next of kin, if the property had descended to them.

(F) As used in this section:

(1) "Trust with powers created by or available to the former spouse" means a trust that is revocable by the former spouse, with respect to which the former spouse has a power of withdrawal, or with respect to which the former spouse may take a distribution that is not subject to an ascertainable standard but does not mean a trust in which those powers of the former spouse are revoked by section 1339.62 of the Revised Code or similar provisions in the law of another state.

(2) "Ascertainable standard" means a standard that is related to a trust beneficiary's health, maintenance, support, or education.

HISTORY: GC §§ 10504-47, 10504-48; 114 v 320(354); Bureau of Code Revision, 10-1-53; 136 v S 145 (Eff 1-1-76); 137 v H 505 (Eff 1-1-79); 141 v S 248. Eff 12-17-86.

§ 2107.34 Afterborn or pretermitted heirs.

If, after making a last will and testament, a testator has a child born alive, or adopts a child, or designates an heir in the manner provided by section 2105.15 of the Revised Code, or if a child or designated heir who is absent and reported to be dead proves to be alive, and no provision has been made in such will or by settlement for such pretermitted child or heir, or for the issue thereof, the will shall not be revoked; but unless it appears by such will that it was the intention of the testator to disinherit such pretermitted child or heir, the devises and legacies granted by such will, except those to a surviving spouse, shall be abated proportionately, or in such other manner as is necessary to give effect to the intention of the testator as shown by the will, so that such pretermitted child or heir will receive a share equal to that which such person would have been entitled to receive out of the estate if such testator had died intestate with no surviving spouse, owning only that portion of his estate not devised or bequeathed to or for the use and benefit of a surviving spouse. If such child or heir dies prior to the death of the testator, the issue of such deceased child or heir shall receive the share the parent would have received if living.

If such pretermitted child or heir supposed to be dead at the time of executing the will has lineal descendants, provision for whom is made by the testator, the other legatees and devisees need not contribute, but such pretermitted child or heir shall take the provision made for his lineal descendants or such part of it as, in the opinion of the probate judge, may be equitable. In settling the claim of a pretermitted child or heir, any portion of the testator's estate received by a party interested, by way of advancement, is a portion of the estate and shall be charged to the party who has received it.

Though measured by sections 2105.01 to 2105.21, inclusive, of the Revised Code, the share taken by a pretermitted child or heir shall be considered as a testate succession. This section does not prejudice the right of any fiduciary to act under any power given by the will, nor shall the title of innocent purchasers for value of any of the property of the testator's estate be affected by any right given by this section to a pretermitted child or heir.

HISTORY: GC § 10504-49; 114 v 320(355); Bureau of Code Revision, 10-1-53; 129 v 7. Eff 10-5-61.

§ 2107.35 Encumbrances.

An encumbrance upon real or personal estate for the purpose of securing the payment of money or the performance of a covenant shall not revoke a will previously executed and relating to such estate.

HISTORY: GC § 10504-50; 114 v 320(356); Bureau of Code Revision, 10-1-53; 127 v 36. Eff 9-4-57.

§ 2107.36 Effect of alteration of property.

An act of a testator which alters but does not wholly divest such testator's interest in property previously devised or bequeathed by him does not revoke the devise or bequest of such property, but such devise or bequest shall pass to the devisee or legatee the actual interest of the testator, which would otherwise descend to his heirs or pass to his next of kin; unless, in the instrument by which such alteration is made, the intention is declared that it shall operate as a revocation of such previous devise or bequest.

If the instrument by which such alteration is made is wholly inconsistent with the previous devise or bequest, such instrument will operate as a revocation thereof, unless such instrument depends on a condition or contingency, and such condition is not performed or such contingency does not happen.

HISTORY: GC §§ 10504-51, 10504-52; 114 v 320(356); Bureau of Code Revision. Eff 10-1-53.

§ 2107.37 Subsequent marriage.

A will executed by an unmarried person is not revoked by a subsequent marriage.

HISTORY: GC § 10504-53; 114 v 320(356); Bureau of Code Revision, 10-1-53; 136 v S 145. Eff 1-1-76.

§ 2107.38 Destruction of a subsequent will.

If a testator executes a second will, the destruction, cancellation, or revocation of the second will shall not revive the first will unless the terms of such revocation show that it was such testator's intention to revive and give effect to his first will or unless, after such destruction, cancellation, or revocation, such testator republishes his first will.

HISTORY: GC § 10504-54; 114 v 320(356); Bureau of Code Revision. Eff 10-1-53.

§ 2107.52 Death of devisee or legatee.

When a devise of real or personal estate is made to a relative of a testator and such relative was dead at the time the will was made, or dies thereafter, leaving issue surviving the testator, such issue shall take the estate devised as the devisee would have done if he had survived the testator. If the testator devised a residuary estate or the entire estate after debts, other legacies and devises, general or specific, or an interest less than a fee or absolute ownership to such devisee and relatives of the testator and such devisee leaves no issue, the estate devised shall vest in such other devisees surviving the testator in such proportions as the testamentary share of each devisee in the devised property bears to the total of the shares of all of the surviving devisees, unless a different disposition is made or required by the will.

HISTORY: GC § 10504-73; 114 v 320(360); Bureau of Code Revision. Eff 10-1-53.

§ 2109.04 Bond.

(A)(1) Unless otherwise provided by law, every fiduciary, prior to the issuance of his letters as provided by section 2109.02 of the Revised Code, shall file in the probate court in which the letters are to be issued a bond with a penal sum in such amount as may be fixed by the court, but in no event less than double the probable value of the personal estate and of the annual real estate rentals which will come into such person's hands as a fiduciary. The bond of a fiduciary shall be in a form approved by the court and signed by two or more personal sureties or by one or more corporate sureties approved by the court. It shall be conditioned that the fiduciary faithfully and honestly will discharge the duties devolving upon him as fiduciary, and shall be conditioned further as may be provided by law.

(2) Except as otherwise provided in this division, if the instrument creating the trust dispenses with the giving of a bond, the court shall appoint a fiduciary without bond, unless the court is of the opinion that the interest of the trust demands it. If the court is of that opinion, it may require bond to be given in any amount it fixes. If a parent nominates a guardian for his child in a will and provides in the will that the guardian may serve without giving bond, the court may appoint the guardian without bond or require the guardian to give bond in accordance with division (A)(1) of this section.

(3) A guardian of the person only does not have to give bond unless, for good cause shown, the court considers a bond to be necessary. When a bond is required of a guardian of the person only, it shall be determined and filed in accordance with division (A)(1) of this section. This division does not apply to a guardian of the person only nominated in a parent's will if the will provides that the guardian may serve without giving bond.

(4) When the probable value of the personal estate and of the annual real estate rentals that will come into the guardian's hands as a fiduciary is less than ten thousand dollars, the court may waive or reduce a bond required by division (A)(1) of this section.

(B) When an executive director who is responsible for the administration of children services in the county is appointed as trustee of the estate of a ward pursuant to section 5153.18 of the Re-

vised Code and has furnished bond under section 5153.13 of the Revised Code, or when an agency under contract with the department of mental retardation and developmental disabilities for the provision of protective service under sections 5123.55 to 5123.59 of the Revised Code is appointed as trustee of the estate of a ward under such sections and any employees of the agency having custody or control of funds or property of such a ward have furnished bond under section 5123.59 of the Revised Code, the court may dispense with the giving of a bond.

(C) When letters are granted without bond, at any later period on its own motion or upon the application of any party interested, the court may require bond to be given in such amount as may be fixed by the court. On failure to give such bond, the defaulting fiduciary shall be removed.

No instrument authorizing a fiduciary whom it names to serve without bond shall be construed to relieve a successor fiduciary from the necessity of giving bond, unless the instrument clearly evidences such intention.

The court by which a fiduciary is appointed may reduce the amount of the bond of such fiduciary at any time for good cause shown.

When two or more persons are appointed as joint fiduciaries, the court may take a separate bond from each or a joint bond from all.

HISTORY: GC §§ 10506-4, 10506-8, 10506-13, 10506-21; 114 v 320 (365-368); 116 v 385; 123 v 534; Bureau of Code Revision, 10-1-53; 125 v 903 (964); 129 v 1623 (Eff 10-5-61); 132 v H 1 (Eff 2-21-67); 134 v H 290 (Eff 3-23-72); 138 v H 900 (Eff 7-1-80); 140 v H 263 (Eff 10-4-84); 143 v S 46 (Eff 1-1-90); 144 v H 82. Eff 9-10-91.

§ 2109.21 Residence qualifications of fiduciary.

(A) An administrator, special administrator, administrator de bonis non, or administrator with the will annexed shall be a resident of this state and shall be removed on proof that he is no longer a resident of this state.

(B)(1) To qualify for appointment as executor or trustee, an executor or a trustee named in a will or nominated in accordance with any power of nomination conferred in a will, may be a resident of this state or, as provided in this division, a nonresident of this state. To qualify for appointment, a nonresident executor or trustee named in, or nominated pursuant to, a will shall be an individual who is related to the maker of the will by consanguinity or affinity, or a person who resides in a state that has statutes or rules that authorize the appointment of a nonresident person who is not related to the maker of a will by consanguinity or affinity, as an executor or trustee when named in, or nominated pursuant to, a will. No such executor or trustee shall be refused appointment or removed solely because he is not a resident of this state.

The court may require that a nonresident executor or trustee named in, or nominated pursuant to, a will assure that all of the assets of the decedent that are in the county at the time of the death of the decedent will remain in the county until distribution or until the court determines that the assets may be removed from the county.

(2) In accordance with this division and section 2129.08 of the Revised Code, the court shall appoint as an ancillary administrator a person who is named in the will of a nonresident decedent, or who is nominated in accordance with any power of nomination conferred in the will of a nonresident decedent, as a general executor of the decedent's estate or as executor of the portion of the decedent's estate located in this state, whether or not the person so named or nominated is a resident of this state.

To qualify for appointment as an ancillary administrator, a person who is not a resident of this state and who is named or nominated as described in this division, shall be an individual who is related to the maker of the will by consanguinity or affinity, or a person who resides in a state that has statutes or rules that authorize the appointment of a nonresident of that state who is not related to the maker of a will by consanguinity or affinity, as an ancillary administrator when the nonresident is named in a will or nominated in accordance with any power of nomination conferred in a will. If a person who is not a resident of this state and who is named or nominated as described in this division so qualifies for appointment as an ancillary administrator and if the provisions of section 2129.08 of the Revised Code are satisfied, the court shall not refuse to appoint the person, and shall not remove the person, as ancillary administrator solely because he is not a resident of this state.

The court may require that an ancillary administrator who is not a resident of this state and who is named or nominated as described in this division, assure that all of the assets of the decedent that are in the county at the time of the death of the decedent will remain in the county until distribution or until the court determines that the assets may be removed from the county.

(C) A guardian shall be a resident of the county, except that the court may appoint a nonresident of the county who is a resident of this state as guardian of the person, the estate, or both; that a nonresident of the county or of this state may be appointed a guardian, if named in a will by a parent of a minor or if selected by a minor over the age of fourteen years as provided by section 2111.12 of the Revised Code; and that a nonresident of the county or of this state may be appointed a guardian if nominated in or pursuant to a durable power of attorney as described in division (D) of section 1337.09 of the Revised Code or a writing as described in division (A) of section 2111.121 [2111.12.1] of the Revised Code. A guardian, other than a guardian named in a will by a parent of a minor, selected by a minor over the age of fourteen years, or nominated in or pursuant to such a durable power of attorney or writing, may be removed on proof that he is no longer a resident of the county in which he resided at the time of his appointment, and shall be removed on proof that he is no longer a resident of this state.

(D) Any fiduciary, whose residence qualifications are not defined in this section, shall be a resident of this state, and shall be removed on proof that he is no longer a resident of this state.

(E) Any fiduciary, in order to assist in the carrying out of his fiduciary duties, may employ agents who are not residents of the county or of this state.

HISTORY: GC § 1056-65; 114 v 320 (378); 123 v 460; Bureau of Code Revision, 10-1-53; 136 v S 145 (Eff 1-1-76); 139 v S 247 (Eff 3-15-83); 140 v S 115 (Eff 10-14-83); 142 v S 228 (Eff 3-22-89); 143 v H 346. Eff 5-31-90.

§ 2109.37 Investment authority.

(A) Except as otherwise provided by law or by the instrument creating the trust, a fiduciary having funds belonging to a trust which are to be invested may invest them in the following:

(1) Bonds or other obligations of the United States or of this state;

(2) Bonds or other interest-bearing obligations of any county, municipal corporation, school district, or other legally constituted political taxing subdivision within the state, provided that such county, municipal corporation, school district, or other subdivision has not defaulted in the payment of the interest on any of its bonds or interest-bearing obligations, for more than one hundred twenty days during the ten years immediately preceding the investment by such fiduciary in such bonds or other obligations, and provided that such county, municipal corporation, school district, or other subdivision, is not, at the time of such investment, in default in the payment of principal or interest on any of its bonds or other interest-bearing obligations;

(3) Bonds or other interest-bearing obligations of any other state of the United States which, within twenty years prior to the making of such investment, has not defaulted for more than ninety days in the payment of principal or interest on any of its bonds or other interest-bearing obligations;

(4) Any bonds issued by or for federal land banks and any debentures issued by or for federal intermediate credit banks under the "Federal Farm Loan Act of 1916," 39 Stat. 360, 12 U.S.C. 641, as amended; or any debentures issued by or for banks for cooperatives under the "Farm Credit Act of 1933," 48 Stat. 257, 12 U.S.C. 131, as amended;

(5) Notes which are: (a) Secured by a first mortgage on real estate held in fee and located in the state, improved by a unit designed principally for residential use for not more than four families or by a combination of such dwelling unit and business property, the area designed or used for nonresidential purposes not to exceed fifty per cent of the total floor area; (b) Secured by a first mortgage on real estate held in fee and located in the state, improved with a building designed for residential use for more than four families or with a building used primarily for business purposes, if the unpaid principal of the notes secured by such mortgage does not exceed ten per cent of the value of the estate or trust or does not exceed five thousand dollars, whichever is greater; or (c) secured by a first mortgage on an improved farm held in fee and located in the state, provided that such mortgage requires that the buildings on the mortgaged property shall be well insured against loss by fire, and so kept, for the benefit of the mortgagee, until the debt is paid, and provided that the unpaid principal of the notes secured by the mortgage shall not exceed fifty per cent of the fair value of the mortgaged real estate at the time

such investment is made, and such notes shall be payable not more than five years after the date on which the investment in them is made; except that the unpaid principal of such notes may equal sixty per cent of the fair value of the mortgaged real estate at the time such investment is made, and may be payable over a period of fifteen years following the date of the investment by the fiduciary if regular installment payments are required sufficient to amortize four per cent or more of the principal of the outstanding notes per annum and if the unpaid principal and interest become due and payable at the option of the holder upon any default in the payment of any installment of interest or principal upon the notes, or of taxes, assessments, or insurance premiums upon the mortgaged premises or upon the failure to cure any such default within any grace period provided therein not exceeding ninety days in duration;

(6) Life, endowment, or annuity contracts of legal reserve life insurance companies regulated by sections 3907.01 to 3907.21, 3909.01 to 3909.17, 3911.01 to 3911.24, 3913.01 to 3913.10, 3915.01 to 3915.15, and 3917.01 to 3917.05 of the Revised Code, and licensed by the superintendent of insurance to transact business within the state, provided that the purchase of contracts authorized by this division shall be limited to executors or the successors to their powers when specifically authorized by will and to guardians and trustees, which contracts may be issued on the life of a ward, a beneficiary of a trust fund, or according to a will, or upon the life of a person in whom such ward or beneficiary has an insurable interest and such contracts shall be drawn by the insuring company so that the proceeds shall be the sole property of the person whose funds are so invested;

(7) Notes or bonds secured by mortgages and insured by the federal housing administrator or debentures issued by such administrator;

(8) Obligations issued by a federal home loan bank created under the "Federal Home Loan Bank Act of 1932," 47 Stat. 725, 12 U.S.C. 11, as amended;

(9) Shares and certificates or other evidences of deposits issued by a federal savings and loan association organized and incorporated under the "Home Owners' Loan Act of 1933," 48 Stat. 128, 12 U.S.C. 1461, as amended, to the extent and only to the extent that those shares or certificates or other evidences of deposits are insured under subchapter IV of the "National Housing Act," 48 Stat. 1246 (1934), 12 U.S.C. 1701, as amended;

(10) Bonds issued by the home owners' loan corporation created under the "Home Owners' Act of 1933," 48 Stat. 128, 12 U.S.C. 1461, as amended;

(11) Obligations issued by the national mortgage association created under the "National Housing Act," 48 Stat. 1246 (1934), 12 U.S.C. 1701, as amended;

(12) Shares and certificates or other evidences of deposits issued by a domestic savings and loan association organized under the laws of the state, which association has obtained insurance of accounts as provided in subchapter IV of the "National Housing Act," 48 Stat. 1246(1934), 12 U.S.C. 1701, as amended, or as may be otherwise provided by law, only to the extent that such evidences of deposits are insured under that act, as amended;

(13) Shares and certificates or other evidences of deposits issued by a domestic savings and loan association organized under the laws of the state, provided that no fiduciary may invest such deposits except with the approval of the probate court, and then in an amount not to exceed the amount which the fiduciary is permitted to invest under division (A)(12) of this section;

(14) In savings accounts in a national bank located in the state or a state bank located in and organized under the laws of the state by depositing such funds in the bank, and such national or state bank when itself acting in a fiduciary

capacity may deposit such funds in savings accounts in its own savings department; provided that no deposit shall be made by any fiduciary, individual, or corporate, unless the deposits of the depository bank are insured by the federal deposit insurance corporation created under the "Federal Deposit Insurance Corporation Act of 1933," 48 Stat. 162, 12 U.S.C. 264, as amended, and provided that the deposit of the funds of any one trust in any such savings accounts in any one bank shall not exceed the sum insured under that act, as amended;

(15) Obligations consisting of notes, bonds, debentures, or equipment trust certificates issued under an indenture, which are the direct obligations, or in the case of equipment trust certificates are secured by direct obligations, of a railroad or industrial corporation, or a corporation engaged directly and primarily in the production, transportation, distribution, or sale of electricity or gas, or the operation of telephone or telegraph systems or waterworks, or in some combination of them; provided that the obligor corporation is one which is incorporated under the laws of the United States, any state, or the district of Columbia, and the obligations are rated at the time of purchase in the highest or next highest classification established by at least two standard rating services selected from a list of the standard rating services which shall be prescribed by the superintendent of banks; provided that every such list shall be certified by such superintendent to the clerk of each probate court in the state, and shall continue in effect until a different list is prescribed and certified as provided in this division;

(16) Obligations issued, assumed, or guaranteed by the international bank for reconstruction and development, the Asian development bank, the inter-American development bank, the African development bank, or other similar development bank in which the president, as authorized by congress and on behalf of the United States, has accepted membership, provided that the obligations are rated at the time of purchase in the highest or next highest classification established by at least one standard rating service selected from a list of standard rating services which shall be prescribed by the superintendent of banks;

(17) Securities of any investment company, as defined in and registered under sections 3 and 8 of the "Investment Company Act of 1940," 54 Stat. 789, 15 U.S.C. 80a-3 and 80a-8, that are invested exclusively in forms of investment or in instruments that are fully collateralized by forms of investment in which the fiduciary is permitted to invest pursuant to divisions (A)(1) to (16) of this section, provided that, in addition to such forms of investment, such investment company may, for the purpose of reducing risk of loss or of stabilizing investment returns, engage in hedging transactions.

(B) No administrator or executor may invest funds belonging to an estate in any asset other than a direct obligation of the United States that has a maturity date not exceeding one year from the date of such investment, or other than in a short-term investment fund that is invested exclusively in obligations of the United States or of its agencies, or primarily in such obligations and otherwise only in variable demand notes, corporate money market instruments including, but not limited to, commercial paper, or fully collateralized repurchase agreements or other evidences of indebtedness that are payable on demand or generally have a maturity date not exceeding ninety-one days from the date of investment, except with the approval of the probate court or with the permission of the instruments creating the trust.

(C)(1) In addition to the investments allowed by this section, a guardian or trustee, with the approval of the court, may invest funds belonging to the trust in productive real estate located within the state, provided that neither the guardian nor the trustee nor any member of the family of either has any interest in such real estate or in the proceeds of the purchase price. The title to any real estate so purchased by a guardian must be taken in the name of the ward.

(2) Notwithstanding the provisions of division (C)(1) of this section, the court may permit the funds to be used to purchase or acquire a home for the ward or an interest in a home for the ward in which a member of the ward's family may have an interest.

HISTORY: GC § 10506-41; 114 v 320(372); 115 v 396; 115 v PtII 284; 116 v 250; 117 v 458; 118 v 503; 119 v 394; 123 v 667; Bureau of Code Revision, 10-1-53; 125 v 903(969); 127 v 27; 128 v 939; 129 v 582(733) (Eff 1-1-61); 131 v 619 (Eff 9-28-65); 131 v 623 (Eff 10-6-65); 133 v S 176 (Eff 10-24-69); 133 v S 171 (Eff 11-6-69); 141 v H 562 (Eff 3-19-86); 142 v H 21 (Eff 10-20-87); 142 v S 228. Eff 3-22-89.

[§ 2109.37.1] § 2109.371
Additional investment authority.

(A) In addition to those investments made eligible by section 2109.37 or 2109.372 [2109.37.2] of the Revised Code, investments may be made by a fiduciary other than a guardian under sections 5905.01 to 5905.19 of the Revised Code, and subject to the restriction placed on an administrator or executor by division (B) of section 2109.37 of the Revised Code, in any of the following kinds and classes of securities, provided that it may be lawfully sold in Ohio and investment is made only in such securities as would be acquired by prudent men of discretion and intelligence in such matters who are seeking a reasonable income and the preservation of their capital:

(1) Securities of corporations organized and existing under the laws of the United States, the District of Columbia, or any state of the United States including, but not limited to, bonds, debentures, notes, equipment trust obligations, or other evidences of indebtedness, and shares of common and preferred stocks of such corporations;

(2) Securities of any open-end or closed-end management type investment company or investment trust, or common trust funds that are established pursuant to section 1109.20 of the Revised Code;

(3) Bonds or other interest-bearing obligations of any state or territory of the United States, or of any county, city, village, school district, or other legally constituted political taxing subdivision of any state or territory of the United States, not otherwise eligible under division (A)(2) or (3) of section 2109.37 of the Revised Code.

(B) No investment shall be made pursuant to this section which, at the time such investment is made, causes the aggregate market value of the investments, not made eligible by section 2109.37 or 2109.372 [2109.37.2] of the Revised Code, to exceed sixty per cent of the aggregate market value at that time of all the property of the fund held by the fiduciary. No sale or other liquidation of any investment shall be required solely because of any change in the relative market value of those investments made eligible by this section and those made eligible by section 2109.37 or 2109.372 [2109.37.2] of the Revised Code; provided that, in the event of a sale of investments authorized by this section, the proceeds from the sale may be reinvested in the kinds and classes of securities authorized by this section without regard to the percentage limitation provided in this division. In determining the aggregate market value of the property of a fund and the percentage of a fund to be invested under this section, a fiduciary may rely upon published market quotations as to those investments for which such quotations are available and upon such valuations of other investments as, in his best judgment, seem fair and reasonable according to available information.

HISTORY: 125 v 812; 129 v 582 (736) (Eff 1-10-61); 131 v 627 (Eff 10-6-65); 132 v H 1 (Eff 2-21-67); 133 v H 655 (Eff 1-1-71); 142 v H 21 (Eff 10-20-87); 142 v H 287 (Eff 10-20-87); 142 v H 708. Eff 4-19-88.

The provisions of § 3 of H 287 (142 v —) read as follows:

SECTION 3. Sections 1109.10, 2109.371, 2109.38, 2109.41, 2109.42, and 5303.27 of the Revised Code, as amended by this act, and sections 1339.44 and 2109.372 of the Revised Code, as enacted by this act, are intended as a declaration and clarification of statutory authority that existed prior to the effective date of this act.

Comment

Ohio's limited or modified "Prudent Man Rule" is patterned after the New York law. See New York Consolidated Laws, Personal Property, § 21.

Revised Code § 2109.37.1 provides that investments may be made by a fiduciary in certain kinds and classes of securities which may be lawfully sold in Ohio, but has stipulated that such investments can be made only in such securities as would be acquired by prudent men of discretion and intelligence in such matters who are seeking a reasonable income and the preservation of THEIR capital.

No administrator or executor, under RC § 2109.37, may invest funds belonging to an estate except with the approval of the court or with the permission of the instrument creating the trust, and hence no administrator or executor may invest funds under RC § 2109.37.1 except with the approval of the court unless the instrument creating the trust permits such investments. Guardians and testamentary trustees may make investments under the provision of RC § 2109.37.1 without court authority. A guardian appointed under the Veterans' Guardianship Law may not invest moneys received from the Veterans' Administration under RC § 2109.37.1. [For additional comment see Addams and Hosford's Ohio Probate Practice.]

[§ 2109.37.2] § 2109.372
When fiduciary may hold cash or make a short term investment.

(A) As used in this section:

(1) "Short term trust-quality investment fund" means a short term investment fund that may be either a registered investment company or a common trust fund established pursuant to section 1109.20 of the Revised Code and that is invested in any one or more of the following manners:

(a) In obligations of the United States or of its agencies;

(b) In obligations of one or more of the states of the United States or their political subdivisions;

(c) In variable demand notes, corporate money market instruments including, but not limited to, commercial paper rated at the time of purchase in either of the two highest classifications established by at least one nationally recognized standard rating service;

(d) Deposits in banks or savings and loan associations whose deposits are insured by the federal deposit insurance corporation or the federal savings and loan insurance corporation if the rate of interest paid on such deposits is at least equal to the rate of interest generally paid by such banks or savings and loan associations on deposits of similar terms or amounts;

(e) In fully collateralized repurchase agreements or other evidences of indebtedness that are of trust quality and are payable on demand or have a maturity date consistent with the purpose of the fund and the duty of fiduciary prudence.

(2) "Registered investment company" means any investment company that is defined in and registered under sections 3 and 8 of the "Investment Company Act of 1940," 54 Stat. 789, 15 U.S.C. 80a-3 and 80a-8.

(B) A fiduciary is not required to invest cash that belongs to the trust and may hold that cash for the period prior to distribution if either of the following applies:

(1) The fiduciary reasonably expects to do either of the following:

(a) Distribute the cash to beneficiaries of the trust on a quarterly or more frequent basis;

(b) Use the cash for the payment of debts, taxes, or expenses of administration within the ninety-day period following the receipt of the cash by the fiduciary.

(2) Determined on the basis of the facilities available to the fiduciary and the amount of the income that reasonably could be earned by the investment of the cash, the amount of the cash does not justify the administrative burden or ex-

pense associated with its investment.

(C) If a fiduciary wishes to hold funds that belong to the trust in liquid form and division (B) of this section does not apply, the fiduciary may so hold the funds as long as they are temporarily invested as described in division (D) of this section.

(D)(1) A fiduciary may make a temporary investment of cash that he may hold uninvested in accordance with division (B) of this section, and shall make a temporary investment of funds held in liquid form pursuant to division (C) of this section, in any of the following investments, unless the governing instrument provides for other investments in which the temporary investment of cash or funds is permitted:

(a) A short term trust-quality investment fund;

(b) Direct obligations of the United States or of its agencies;

(c) A deposit with a bank or savings and loan association whose deposits are insured by the federal deposit insurance corporation or the federal savings and loan insurance corporation, if the rate of interest paid on that deposit is at least equal to the rate of interest generally paid by that bank or savings and loan association on deposits of similar terms or amounts.

(2) A fiduciary that makes a temporary investment of cash or funds pursuant to division (D)(1) of this section may charge a reasonable fee for the services associated with that investment. The fee shall be in addition to the compensation to which the fiduciary is entitled for his ordinary fiduciary services.

(3) Fiduciaries that make one or more temporary investments of cash or funds pursuant to division (D)(1) of this section shall provide to the beneficiaries of the trusts involved, that are currently receiving income or have a right to receive income, a written disclosure of their temporary investment practices and, if applicable, the method of computing reasonable fees for their temporary investment services pursuant to division (D)(2) of this section. Fiduciaries may comply with this requirement in any appropriate written document, including, but not limited to, any periodic statement or account.

HISTORY: 142 v H 287 (Eff 10-20-87); 142 v H 503. Eff 9-9-88.

See provisions, § 3 of H 287 (142 v —), following RC § 2109.37.1.

§ 2109.67 Expenses charged against principal; distribution of income.

(A) Unless the will otherwise provides and subject to division (B) of this section, all expenses incurred in connection with the settlement of a decedent's estate, including debts, funeral expenses, estate taxes, penalties concerning taxes, allowances to a surviving spouse, minor children, or both, including, but not limited to, the allowance for support under section 2106.13 of the Revised Code, fees of attorneys and personal representatives, and court costs shall be charged against the principal of the estate.

(B) Unless the will otherwise provides, income from the assets of a decedent's estate after the death of the testator and before distribution, including income from property used to discharge liabilities, shall be determined in accordance with the rules applicable to a trustee under Chapter 1340. of the Revised Code and distributed as follows:

(1) To specific legatees and devisees, the income from the property bequeathed or devised to them respectively, less property taxes, ordinary repairs, interest, and other expenses of management and operation of the property, and an appropriate portion of taxes imposed on income, excluding taxes on capital gains, income in respect of a decedent, and other items allocable to principal, which accrue during the period of administration;

(2) To all other legatees, except as provided in division (B)(3) of this section,

the balance of the income, less the balance of property taxes, ordinary repairs, interest, and other expenses of management and operation of all property from which the estate is entitled to income, and taxes imposed on income, excluding taxes on capital gains, income in respect of a decedent, and other items allocable to principal, which accrue during the period of administration, in proportion to their respective interests in the undistributed assets of the estate, computed at times of distribution on the basis of inventory value;

(3) A legatee, other than the testator's surviving spouse, of a pecuniary legacy not in trust shall not be paid interest on the legacy, and the legacy shall not be entitled to receive any part of the income received by the estate during the period of administration as income on the legacy. A legacy to the testator's surviving spouse of a pecuniary amount shall carry with it a proportionate part of the income of the estate from the testator's death to the date of satisfaction, determined in accordance with division (B)(2) of this section.

HISTORY: 142 v S 146 (Eff 10-20-87); 143 v H 346. Eff 5-31-90.

§ 2111.12 Guardian of minor.

A minor over the age of fourteen years may select a guardian who shall be appointed if a suitable person. If such minor fails to select a suitable person, an appointment may be made without reference to his wishes. The minor shall not select one person to be the guardian of his estate only and another to be the guardian of the person only, unless the court which appoints is of the opinion that the interests of such minor will thereby be promoted.

A surviving parent by last will in writing may appoint a guardian for any of his children, whether born at the time of making the will or afterward, to continue during the minority of the child or for a less time.

When the father or mother of a minor names a person as guardian of the estate of such minor in a will, the person named shall have preference in appointment over the person selected by such minor. A person named in such will as guardian of the person of such minor shall have no preference in appointment over the person selected by such minor, but in such event the probate court may appoint the person named in the will, the person selected by the minor, or some other person.

Whenever a testamentary guardian is appointed, his duties, powers, and liabilities in all other respects shall be governed by the law regulating guardians not appointed by will.

HISTORY: GC §§ 10507-12—10507-14; 114 v 320(386); 121 v 557(570); Bureau of Code Revision. Eff 10-1-53.

§ 2113.03 Release from administration.

(A) Upon the application of any interested party, after notice of the filing of the application has been given to the surviving spouse and heirs at law in the manner and for the length of time the probate court directs, and after three weeks' notice to all interested parties by publication once each week in a newspaper of general circulation in the county, unless the notices are waived or found unnecessary, the court, when satisfied that the assets of an estate are twenty-five thousand dollars or less in value, and that creditors will not be prejudiced, may make an order relieving the estate from administration and directing delivery of personal property and transfer of real estate to the persons entitled to them.

For the purposes of this section, the value of an estate that can reasonably be considered to approximate twenty-five thousand dollars or less, and that is not composed entirely of money, stocks, bonds, or other property the value of which is readily ascertainable, shall be determined by an appraiser selected by the applicant, subject to the approval of the court. The appraiser's valuation of the property shall be reported to the court in the application to relieve the estate from administration. The appraiser shall be paid in accordance with section 2115.06 of the Revised Code.

For the purposes of this section, the amount of property to be delivered or transferred to the surviving spouse, minor children, or both of the deceased as the allowance for support, shall be established in accordance with section 2106.13 of the Revised Code.

When a delivery, sale, or transfer of personal property has been ordered from an estate that has been relieved from administration, the court may appoint a commissioner to execute all necessary instruments of conveyance. The commissioner shall receipt for the property, distribute the proceeds of the conveyance upon court order, and report to the court after distribution.

When the decedent died testate, the will shall be presented for probate, and, if admitted to probate, the court may relieve the estate from administration and order distribution of the estate under the will.

An order of the court relieving an estate from administration shall have the same effect as administration proceedings in freeing land in the hands of an innocent purchaser for value from possible claims of unsecured creditors.

(B) An application to relieve an estate from administration shall be in writing and shall contain the following information:

(1) The name, date of death, and place of residence at the time of death, of the decedent;

(2) The name of the surviving spouse of the decedent, and the names, ages, and addresses of the persons entitled to the next estate of inheritance under the statutes of descent and distribution, and their respective degrees of relationship to the decedent and to the surviving spouse of the decedent;

(3) A summary statement of the character and value of the property comprising the estate;

(4) A list of all known creditors of the decedent, and the amount of their claims;

(5) If the decedent died testate or intestate, a statement to that effect.

(C) The application shall be in the following form, and this form shall be used exclusively by the probate courts in this state:

"Application for Release of Estate from Administration
Revised Code, Sec. 2113.03

No . . . Doc . . . Page . . . Filed . . ., 19. .
Common Pleas Court, Probate Division, County, Ohio

In the Matter of)
THE ESTATE OF)   No. . . . .
.............................)   . . . ., 19. . .
          Deceased   )

. . . . says that . . . . late a resident of the . . . . . . of . . . ., ... County, Ohio, died . . . .
                                        (testate
                                            or
                                        intestate)
on the . . . . day of . . . ., 19 . . ., leaving . . . . surviving spouse, and the following persons entitled to the next estate of inheritance under the statutes of descent and distribution whose names, ages, respective degrees of relationship to the decedent, relationship to the surviving spouse of the decedent, and addresses are as follows:

Name	Age	Relationship to Decedent	Relationship to Surviving Spouse of Decedent	Address

The applicant selects . . . . to act when required, as appraiser of the real and personal property of the decedent, the value of which is not readily ascertainable.

The following is a summary statement of the character and value of the property comprising the estate.

Appraiser's Report:

I certify that the foregoing is a true and correct appraisement of the property exhibited to me.

Dated . . . . , 19. . .   . .
                                                    Appraiser

RECAPITULATION OF ASSETS

Personal Property of the value of $ . . . .
Real Estate of the value of . . . . $ . . . .
                                    _____
                    Total Estate $ . . . . . .

That the debts owing by the decedent and to whom owing are as follows:

Name	Address	For What	Amount

The estate being $25,000 or less in amount, the applicant asks that the estate be relieved from administration and that delivery or transfer of the property be made to the following persons:

Name	Address	Property to be Delivered or Transferred

. . . .
                                    Applicant

WAIVER

We the undersigned, surviving spouse and heirs at law of the above named decedent and interested parties in the above entitled action hereby waive service of notice in the above entitled action and consent to the delivery or transfer of the described property as prayed for above.

Dated this . . . .   day of . . . ., 19. . .

. . . .
. . . .
. . . .
. . . .
. . . .
. . . .

ORDER RELIEVING ESTATE FROM ADMINISTRATION

The court finds that the decedent died on . . . ., 19. . ., and that the entire estate of the decedent consists of assets having the value of $ . . . . ..

The court finds from the representations made that further notice is unnecessary, that the estate is within the provisions of section 2113.03 of the Revised Code, and that creditors will not be prejudiced by granting the order. It is therefore ordered and decreed that the estate be and hereby is relieved from administration, and it is further ordered that the property of the estate be delivered and transferred to the following persons:

Name	Address	Property to be Delivered or Transferred

. . . .
                    Probate Judge.''

HISTORY: GC § 10509-5; 114 v 320 (402); 116 v 385; 122 v 427; Bureau of Code Revision, 10-1-53; 130 v 615 (Eff 9-24-63); 132 v H 68 (12-11-67); 134 v S 54 (12-13-71); 135 v S 25 (Eff 11-21-73); 136 v S 145 (Eff 1-1-76); 136 v S 466 (Eff 5-26-76); 142 v H 21 (Eff 10-20-87); 143 v H 346. Eff 5-31-90.

§ 2113.05 Letters testamentary shall issue.

When a will is approved and allowed, the probate court shall issue letters testamentary to the executor named in the will or to the executor nominated by holders of a power as described in section 2107.65 of the Revised Code, or to the executor named in the will and to a coexecutor nominated by holders of such a power, if he is suitable, competent, accepts the appointment, and gives bond if that is required.

If no executor is named in a will and no power as described in section 2107.65 of the Revised Code is conferred in the will, or if the executor named in a will or nominated pursuant to such a power dies, fails to accept the appointment, resigns, or is otherwise disqualified and the holders of such a power do not have authority to nominate another executor or no such power is conferred in the will, or if such a power is conferred in a will but the power cannot be exercised because of the death of a holder of the power, letters of administration with the will annexed shall be granted to a suitable person or persons, named as devisees or legatees in the will, who would have been entitled to administer the estate if the decedent had died intestate, unless the will indicates an intention that the person or persons shall not be granted letters of administration. Otherwise, the court shall grant letters of administration with the will annexed to some other suitable person.

HISTORY: GC § 10509-2; 114 v 320(401); 116 v 385; Bureau of Code Revision, 10-1-53; 125 v 903 (974) (Eff 10-1-53); 133 v S 134 (Eff 6-12-70); 136 v S 145 (Eff 1-1-76); 139 v S 247 (Eff 3-15-83); 140 v S 115. Eff 10-14-83.

§ 2113.06 To whom letters of administration shall be granted.

Administration of the estate of an intestate shall be granted to persons mentioned in this section, in the following order:

(A) To the surviving spouse of the deceased, if resident of the state;

(B) To one of the next of kin of the deceased, resident of the state.

If the persons entitled to administer the estate fail to take or renounce administration voluntarily, they shall be cited by the probate court for that purpose.

If there are no persons entitled to administration, or if they are for any reason unsuitable for the discharge of the trust, or if without sufficient cause they neglect to apply within a reasonable time for the administration of the estate, their right to priority shall be lost, and the court shall commit the administration to some suitable person who is a resident of the state. Such person may be a creditor of the estate.

This section applies to the appointment of an administrator de bonis non.

HISTORY: GC § 10509-3; 114 v 320(401); 116 v 385; Bureau of Code Revision, 10-1-53; 136 v S 145 (Eff 1-1-76); 136 v S 466. Eff 5-26-76.

§ 2113.12 Procedure if executor renounces.

If a person named as executor in the will of a decedent, or nominated as an executor by holders of a power as described in section 2107.65 of the Revised Code, refuses to accept the trust, or, if after being cited for that purpose, neglects to appear and accept, or if he neglects for twenty days after the probate of the will to give any required bond, the probate court shall grant letters testamentary to the other executor, if there is one capable and willing to accept the trust, and if there is no such other executor named in the will or nominated by holders of a power as described in section 2107.65 of the Revised Code, the court shall commit administration of the estate, with the will annexed, to some suitable and competent person, pursuant to section 2113.05 of the Revised Code.

HISTORY: GC § 10509-10; 114 v 320(403); 116 v 385; Bureau of Code Revision, 10-1-53; 133 v S 134 (Eff 6-12-70); 140 v S 115. Eff 10-14-83.

§ 2113.15 Special administrator.

When there is delay granting letters testamentary or of administration, the probate court may appoint a special administrator to collect and preserve the effects of the deceased.

Such special administrator must collect the chattels and debts of the deceased and preserve them for the executor or administrator who thereafter is appointed. For that purpose such special administrator may begin and maintain suits as administrator and also sell such goods as the court orders sold. He shall be allowed such compensation for his services as the court thinks reasonable, if he forthwith delivers the property and effects of the estate to the executor or administrator who supersedes him.

HISTORY: GC §§ 10509-14, 10509-15; 114 v 320(403, 404); Bureau of Code Revision. Eff 10-1-53.

§ 2113.19 Administrator de bonis non.

When a sole executor or administrator dies without having fully administered the estate, the probate court shall grant letters of administration, with the will annexed or otherwise as the case requires, to some suitable person pursuant to section 2113.05 or 2113.06 of the Revised Code. Such person shall administer the goods and estate of the deceased not administered, in case there is personal estate to be administered to the amount of twenty dollars or debts to that amount due from the estate.

HISTORY: GC § 10509-20; 114 v 320(404); Bureau of Code Revision, 10-1-53; 133 v S 134. Eff 6-12-70.

§ 2113.25 Assets to be collected.

So far as he is able, the executor or administrator of an estate shall collect the assets and complete the administration of such estate within nine months after the date of his appointment.

Upon application of the executor or administrator and notice to the interested parties, if the probate court deems such notice necessary, the court may allow further time in which to collect assets, to convert assets into money, to pay creditors, to make distributions to legatees or distributees, to file partial, final, and distributive accounts, and to settle estates. The court, upon application of any interested party, may authorize the examination under oath in open court of the executor or administrator upon any matter relating to the administration of the estate.

HISTORY: GC §§ 10509-85, 10509-86; 114 v 32()(420); 119 v 394(406); Bureau of Code Revision. Eff 10-1-53.

§ 2113.26 Contents of application.

An application made by an executor or administrator under section 2113.25 of the Revised Code shall set forth the grounds of the application, the amount of money in the hands of the executor or administrator applicable on the debts of the deceased, and that he has used due diligence in performing the duties enumerated therein. Such application shall be supported by the affidavit of the executor or administrator.

HISTORY: GC § 10509-87; 114 v 320(420); 119 v 394(406); Bureau of Code Revision. Eff 10-1-53.

§ 2113.27 Extension of time limited.

The probate court shall not at any one time grant an extension of more than six months from the date of application under sections 2113.25 and 2113.26 of the Revised Code, except that in cases where the estate is subject to estate or inheritance taxes which cannot be determined and paid within six months, the court may grant an extension for such longer period as it deems proper. The office of the executor or administrator shall not cease with the time allowed by law or the court for the performance of the duties enumerated in such sections.

HISTORY: GC § 10509-88; 114 v 320(420); 119 v 394(406); Bureau of Code Revision. Eff 10-1-53.

§ 2113.28 Time allowed to collect assets not to defer account.

The time allowed by the probate court to collect the assets of an estate shall not operate as an allowance of further time to file the accounts required by section 2109.30 of the Revised Code.

HISTORY: GC § 10509-171; 114 v 320(439); Bureau of Code Revision. Eff 10-1-53.

§ 2113.30 Continuing decedent's business.

Except as otherwise directed by the decedent in his last will and testament, an executor or administrator may, without personal liability for losses incurred, continue the decedent's business during one month next following the date of the appointment of such executor or administrator, unless the probate court directs otherwise, and for such further time as the court may authorize on hearing and after notice to the surviving spouse and distributees. In either case no debts incurred or contracts entered into shall involve the estate beyond the assets used in such business immediately prior to the death of the decedent without the approval of the court first obtained. During the time the business is continued, the executor or administrator shall file monthly reports in the court, setting forth the receipts and expenses of the business for the preceding month and such other pertinent information as the court may require. The executor or administrator may not bind the estate without court approval beyond the period during which the business is continued.

HISTORY: GC § 10509-9; 114 v 320(402); 116 v 385; Bureau of Code Revision. Eff 10-1-53.

§ 2113.31 Responsibility of executor or administrator.

Every executor or administrator is chargeable with all chattels, rights, and credits of the deceased which come into his hands and are to be administered, although not included in the inventory required by section 2115.02 of the Revised Code. Such executor or administrator is also chargeable with all the proceeds of personal property and real estate sold for the payment of debts or legacies, and all the interest, profit, and income that in any way comes to his hands from the personal estate of the deceased.

HISTORY: GC § 10509-172; 114 v 320(439); Bureau of Code Revision. Eff 10-1-53.

[§ 2113.31.1] § 2113.311 Management of real estate by executor or administrator.

(A) If, within a reasonable time after the appointment of the executor or administrator, no one in authority has taken over the management and rental of any real estate of which the decedent died seized, the executor or administrator, or an heir or devisee may, unless the will otherwise provides, make application to the probate court for an order authorizing the executor or administrator to assume such duties. Such application shall contain:

(1) A brief statement of the facts upon which the application is based and such other pertinent information as the court may require;

(2) A description or identification of the real estate and the interest owned by the decedent at the time of his death;

(3) The names and addresses, if known to the applicant, of the persons to whom such real estate passed by descent or devise.

Notice of the time of hearing on such application shall be given to the persons designated in sub-paragraph division (A)(3) of this section, unless for good cause the court dispenses with such notice, and also to the executor or administrator, unless the executor or administrator is the applicant.

If the court finds that the statements contained in the application are true and that it would be for the best interest of such heirs or devisees that the application be granted, it may authorize the executor or administrator to assume the management and rental of such real estate.

The court may require bond, new or additional, in an amount to be fixed by the court and conditioned that the executor or administrator will faithfully and honestly discharge the duties devolving upon him by the provisions of this section.

(B) In the exercise of such authority, the executor of administrator shall be authorized to do the following:

(1) Collect rents;

(2) From the rents collected:

(a) Pay all taxes and assessments due on such real estate, and all such usual operating expenses in connection with the management thereof;

(b) Make repairs when necessary to preserve such real estate from waste, provided that an order of the court shall first be obtained if the cost of such repairs exceeds one hundred dollars;

(c) Insure buildings against loss by fire or other casualty and against public liability;

(3) Advance money upon an order first obtained from the court, for such repairs, taxes, insurance, and all usual operating expenses, which shall be a charge on such real estate;

(4) Rent the property on a month to month basis, or, upon an order first obtained from the court, for a period not to exceed one year;

(5) Prosecute actions for forcible entry and detention of such real estate.

The executor or administrator shall, at intervals not to exceed twelve months, pay over to the heirs or devisees, if known, their share of the net rents, and shall account for all money received and paid out under authority of this section in his regular accounts of the administration of the estate, but in a separate schedule. If any share of the net rents remains unclaimed, it may be disposed of in the same manner as is provided for unclaimed money under section 2113.64 of the Revised Code.

The authority granted under this section shall terminate upon the transfer of the real estate to the heirs or devisees in accordance with section 2113.61 of the Revised Code, or upon a sale thereof, or upon application of the executor or administrator, or for a good cause shown, upon the application of an heir or devisee.

Upon application the court may allow compensation to the executor or administrator for extraordinary services, which shall be charged against the rents, and if said rents be insufficient, shall be a charge against such real estate.

Upon application the court may allow reasonable attorney fees paid by the executor or administrator when an attorney is employed in connection with the management and rental of such real estate, which shall be charged against the rents, and if said rents be insufficient, shall be a charge against such real estate.

HISTORY: 128 v 76, § 1. Eff 11-9-59.

§ 2113.32 Executors and administrators not to profit.

No profits shall be made by executors or administrators by the increase of any part of an estate, nor shall they sustain any loss by the decrease or destruction of such estate without their fault.

HISTORY: GC § 10509-173; 114 v 320(440); Bureau of Code Revision. Eff 10-1-53.

§ 2113.33 Not responsible for bad debts.

An executor or administrator is not accountable for debts inventoried as due to the decedent, if it appears to the probate court that, without his fault, they remain uncollected.

HISTORY: GC § 10509-174; 114 v 320(440); Bureau of Code Revision. Eff 10-1-53.

§ 2113.34 Chargeable with property consumed.

If an executor or administrator neglects to sell personal property which he is required to sell, and retains, consumes, or disposes of it for his own benefit, he shall be charged therewith at double the value affixed thereto by the appraisers.

HISTORY: GC § 10509-175; 114 v 320(440); Bureau of Code Revision, 10-1-53; 125 v 903(975). Eff 10-1-53.

§ 2113.35 Commissions.

Executors and administrators shall be allowed commissions upon the amount of all the personal estate, including the income from the personal estate, that is received and accounted for by them and upon the proceeds of real estate that is sold as follows:

(A) For the first one hundred thousand dollars, at the rate of four per cent;

(B) All above one hundred thousand dollars and not exceeding four hundred thousand dollars, at the rate of three per cent;

(C) All above four hundred thousand dollars, at the rate of two per cent.

Executors and administrators also shall be allowed a commission of one per cent on the value of real estate that is not sold. Executors and administrators also shall be allowed a commission of one per cent on all property that is not subject to administration and that is includable for purposes of computing the Ohio estate tax, except joint and survivorship property.

The basis of valuation for the allowance of such commissions on real estate sold shall be the gross proceeds of sale, and for all other property the fair market value of the other property as of the date of death of the decedent. The commissions allowed to executors and administrators in this section shall be received in full compensation for all their ordinary services.

If the probate court finds, after hearing, that an executor or administrator, in any respect, has not faithfully discharged his duties as executor or administrator, the court may deny the executor or administrator any compensation whatsoever or may allow the executor or administrator the reduced compensation that the court thinks proper.

HISTORY: GC § 10509-192; 114 v 320 (443); 116 v 385 (402); 119 v 394 (416); Bureau of Code Revision, 10-1-53; 135 v H 691 (Eff 6-19-74); 138 v S 158 (Eff 7-30-80); 143 v H 346. Eff 5-31-90.

§ 2113.36 Further allowance; counsel fees.

Allowances, in addition to those provided by section 2113.35 of the Revised Code for an executor or administrator, which the probate court considers just and reasonable shall be made for actual and necessary expenses and for extraordinary services not required of an executor or administrator in the common course of his duty.

Upon the application of an executor or administrator for further allowances for extraordinary services rendered, the court shall review both ordinary and extraordinary services claimed to have been rendered. If the commissions payable pursuant to section 2113.35 of the Revised Code, exceed the reasonable value of such ordinary services rendered, the court must adjust any allowance made for extraordinary services so that total commissions and allowances to be made fairly reflect the reasonable value of both ordinary and extraordinary services.

When an attorney has been employed in the administration of the estate, reasonable attorney fees paid by the executor or administrator shall be allowed as a part of the expenses of administration. The court may at any time during administration fix the amount of such fees and, on application of the executor or administrator or the attorney, shall fix the amount thereof. When provision is made by the will of the deceased for compensation to an executor, the amount provided shall be a full satisfaction for his services, in lieu of such commissions or his share thereof, unless by an instrument filed in the court within four months after his appointment he renounces all claim to the compensation given by the will.

HISTORY: GC § 10509-193; 114 v 320(443); 119 v 394(416); Bureau of Code Revision, 10-1-53; 135 v H 691. Eff 6-19-74.

§ 2113.37 Allowance for tombstone and cemetery lot.

The probate court in settlement of an executor's or administrator's account may allow as a credit to the executor or administrator a just amount expended by him for a tombstone or monument for the deceased and a just amount paid by him to a cemetery association or corporation as a perpetual fund for caring for and preserving the lot on which the deceased is buried. It is not incumbent on an executor or administrator to procure a tombstone or monument or to pay any sum into such fund.

HISTORY: GC § 10509-178; 114 v 320(440); Bureau of Code Revision. Eff 10-1-53.

§ 2113.39 Sale of property under authority of will.

If a qualified executor, administrator, or testamentary trustee is authorized by will or devise to sell any class of personal property whatsoever or real estate, no order shall be required from the probate court to enable him to act in pursuance of the power vested in him. A power to sell authorizes a sale for any purpose deemed by such executor, administrator, or testamentary trustee to be for the best interest of the estate, unless the power is expressly limited by such will.

HISTORY: GC § 10509-227; 114 v 320(451); 122 v 497; Bureau of Code Revision. Eff 10-1-53.

§ 2113.40 Sale of personal property.

At any time after the appointment of an executor or administrator, the probate court, when satisfied that it would be for the best interests of the estate, may authorize such executor or administrator to sell at public or private sale, at a fixed price or for the best price obtainable, and for cash or on such terms as the court may determine, any part or all of the personal property belonging to the estate, except:

(A) Such property as the surviving spouse desires to take at the appraised value;

(B) Property specifically bequeathed, when sale of such property is not necessary for the payment of debts, provided that such property may be sold with the consent of the person entitled thereto, including executors, administrators, guardians, and trustees;

(C) Property as to which distribution in kind has been demanded prior to the sale by the surviving spouse or other beneficiary entitled to such distribution in kind;

(D) Property which the court directs shall not be sold pursuant to a wish expressed by the decedent in his will; but at any later period, on application of a party interested, the court may, and for good cause shall, require such sale to be made.

In case of sale before expiration of the time within which the surviving spouse may elect to take at the appraised value, not less than ten days' notice of such sale shall be given to the surviving spouse, unless such surviving spouse consents to such sale or waives notice thereof. Such notice shall not be required as to perishable property.

The court may permit the itemized list of personal property being sold to be incorporated in documents and records relating to the sale, by reference to other documents and records which have been filed in the court. Provided that a court order shall not be required to permit the public sale of personal goods and chattels.

HISTORY: GC § 10509-90; 114 v 320(421); Bureau of Code Revision. Eff 10-1-53.

§ 2113.41 Public sale.

Public sales of personal property mentioned in section 2113.40 of the Revised Code shall be at public auction and, unless otherwise directed by the probate court, after notice of such sale has been given:

(A) By advertisement appearing at least three times in a newspaper of general circulation in the county during a period of fifteen days next preceding such sale;

(B) By advertisement posted not less than fifteen days next preceding such sale in at least five public places in the township or municipal corporation where such sale is to take place;

(C) By both such forms of advertisement.

Such advertisement published or posted shall specify generally the property to be sold and the date, place, and terms of sale. The executor or administrator, if he deems it for the best interests of the estate may employ an auctioneer or clerk, or both, to conduct such sale, and their reasonable fees and charges shall be deducted from the proceeds of the sale. The court for good cause may extend the time for sale.

HISTORY: GC § 10509-91; 114 v 320(421); Bureau of Code Revision, 10-1-53; 125 v 903(976). Eff 10-1-53.

§ 2113.42 Report of sale.

Within thirty days after any public or private sale of the personal property of an estate, the executor or administrator shall make report thereof to the probate court. Such report shall include proof of proper notice of such sale, if at public auction, and, if a clerk was employed for such sale shall be accompanied by a sale bill signed by such clerk. The report of sale shall be sworn to by the executor or administrator.

HISTORY: GC § 10509-92; 114 v 320(422); Bureau of Code Revision. Eff 10-1-53.

§ 2113.43 Credit.

In all sales of the personal property of an estate the probate court may authorize the executor or administrator to sell on credit, the unpaid purchase price to be secured by notes or bonds with two or more sureties and approved by the executor or administrator. An executor or administrator shall not be responsible for loss due to the insolvency of the purchaser of any of such property if it appears that such executor or administrator acted with caution in extending credit pursuant to the authority of the court and has diligently tried to collect such notes and bonds.

HISTORY: GC § 10509-93; 114 v 320(422); Bureau of Code Revision. Eff 10-1-53.

§ 2113.44 Sale of notes secured by mortgage.

An executor or administrator, without court order, may sell and transfer, without recourse, any promissory notes secured by mortgage and the mortgage securing such notes at not less than the face value thereof with accrued interest.

HISTORY: GC § 10509-94; 114 v 320(422); Bureau of Code Revision. Eff 10-1-53.

§ 2113.51 Property may be delivered to legatee.

The property of an estate which is specifically bequeathed may be delivered over to the legatee entitled thereto. Such legatee must secure its redelivery on demand to the executor or administrator. Otherwise, such property must remain in the hands of the executor or administrator to be distributed or sold, as required by law and the condition of the estate.

HISTORY: GC § 10509-180; 114 v 320(441); Bureau of Code Revision. Eff 10-1-53.

§ 2113.52 Devisee takes subject to tax lien; exoneration of mortgage lien.

(A) A devisee taking real estate under a devise in a will, unless the will otherwise provides, or an heir taking real estate under the statutes of descent and distribution shall take the real estate subject to all taxes, penalties, interest, and assessments which are a lien against that real estate.

(B) If real estate devised in a will is subject to a mortgage lien that exists on the date of the testator's death, the person taking the real estate under the devise has no right of exoneration for the mortgage lien, regardless of a general direction in the will to pay the testator's debts, unless the will specifically provides a right of exoneration that extends to that lien.

HISTORY: GC § 10509-122b; 119 v 394(423), § 7; Bureau of Code Revision, 10-1-53; 125 v 903(977) (Eff 10-1-53); 139 v H 379 (Eff 9-21-82); 140 v S 115. Eff 10-14-83.

§ 2113.53 Distribution of assets of estate.

At any time after the appointment of an executor or administrator, the executor or administrator may distribute to the beneficiaries entitled to assets of the estate under the will, if there is no action pending to set aside the will, or to the heirs entitled to assets of the estate by law, in cash or in kind, any part or all of the assets of the estate. Each beneficiary or heir is liable to return the assets, or the proceeds from the assets, if they are necessary to satisfy the share of a surviving spouse who elects to take against the will pursuant to section 2106.01 of the Revised Code, or to satisfy any claims against the estate. If any executor or administrator distributes any part of the assets of the estate before the expiration of the times described in division (E) of section 2106.01 of the Revised Code for the making of an election by a surviving spouse, he is personally liable to any surviving spouse who subsequently elects to take against the will. If the executor or administrator distributes any part of the assets of the estate within three months after the death of the decedent, the executor or administrator is personally liable only to those claimants who present their claims within that three-month period. If the executor or administrator distributes any part of the assets of the estate more than three months but less than one year after the death of the decedent, the executor or administrator is personally liable only to those claimants who present their claims before the distribution. If the executor or administrator distributes any part of the assets of the estate more than one year after the death of the decedent, he is personally liable only to those claimants who present their claims within one year after the death of the decedent. The executor or administrator shall be liable only to the extent a claim is finally allowed.

The executor or administrator shall be liable only to the extent that the sum of the remaining assets of the estate and the assets returned by the beneficiaries or heirs is insufficient to satisfy the share of the surviving spouse and to satisfy the claims against the estate. The executor or administrator shall not be liable in any case for an amount greater than the value of the estate that existed at the time that the distribution of assets was made and that was subject to the spouse's share or to the claims.

Any executor or administrator may provide for the payment of rejected claims or claims in suit by setting aside a sufficient amount of the assets of the estate for paying the claims. The assets shall be set aside for the payment of the claims in a manner approved by the probate court. Each claimant for whom assets are to be set aside shall be given notice, in the manner as the court shall order, of the hearing upon the application to set aside assets and shall have the right to be fully heard as to the nature and amount of the assets to be set aside for payment of his claim and as to all other conditions in connection with the claim. In any case in which the executor or administrator may set aside assets as provided in this section, the court, upon its own motion or upon application of the executor or administrator, as a condition precedent to any distribution, may require any beneficiary or heir to give a bond to the state with surety approved and in an amount fixed by the court, conditioned to secure the return of the assets to be distributed, or the proceeds from the assets or as much of the assets as may be necessary to satisfy the claims that may be recovered against the estate, and to indemnify the executor or administrator against loss and damage on account of such distribution. The bond may be in addition to the assets to be set aside or partially or wholly in lieu of the assets, as the court shall determine.

HISTORY: GC § 10509-181; 114 v 320 (441); 119 v 394 (414); Bureau of Code Revision, 10-1-53; 133 v S 185 (Eff 1-1-71); 136 v S 145 (Eff 1-1-76); 143 v H 346. Eff 5-31-90.

[§ 2113.53.1] § 2113.531
Interest on general legacies.

General legacies shall bear no interest unless specifically provided in the will.
HISTORY: 127 v 381. Eff 9-4-57.

[§ 2113.53.3] § 2113.533
Notice of distribution of assets prior to deadline for claims against estate.

(A) If the executor or administrator distributes any part of the assets of the estate prior to the expiration of the time period for the filing of claims against the estate as set forth in section 2117.06 of the Revised Code, he shall send a notice to the distributee prior to that distribution. The executor or administrator shall pay out of the estate the costs associated with the preparation and mailing of the notice. The notice shall contain the following information:

(1) The county of probate, the probate case number, and the name of the estate of the deceased;

(2) The date of the notice and the address of the executor or administrator;

(3) A statement that informs the distributee that the distribution of the assets is being made before the expiration of the deadline for the filing of claims against the estate as set forth in section 2117.06 of the Revised Code, and for that reason the distributee may be liable to the estate up to the value of the distribution and may be required to return all or any part of the value of the distribution he receives if a valid claim is subsequently made against the estate within the time permitted under section 2117.06 of the Revised Code.

(B) The notice shall include a signature line for the distributee preceded by a statement that the distributee received the notice and acknowledges that he may be required to return to the estate the value of the distribution he receives.

(C) Until the supreme court, pursuant to its powers of superintendence under Section 5, Article IV of the Ohio Constitution, develops and adopts a form to govern the notice required under divisions (A) and (B) of this section, a form substantially as follows shall be used:

"Probate Court of . . . . . . County, Ohio

Estate of . . . ., Deceased
Case No. . . . ., Docket . . . ., Page . . . .

NOTICE TO DISTRIBUTEE
The executor or administrator of the estate of .... is making a distribution to you of the assets of the above-described estate prior to the expiration of the deadline for the filing of claims against the estate as set forth in

section 2117.06 of the Revised Code. Therefore you may be liable to the estate up to the value of the distribution and may be required as a distributee to return all or any part of the value of the distribution you receive if a valid claim is subsequently made against the estate within the time permitted under section 2117.06 of the Revised Code.

Name of executor or administrator ......
Address of executor or administrator ..
I acknowledge that I have read the above notice and I understand that I may be required to return any or all of the value of the distribution I receive at this time prior to the expiration of the deadline for the filing of claims against the estate. Distributee.................. Date ...."

HISTORY: 143 v H 346. Eff 5-31-90.

§ 2113.54 Distribution upon application of legatee or distributee.

When five months have expired after the appointment of an executor or administrator and the surviving spouse has made an election under section 2106.01 of the Revised Code, a legatee or distributee may apply to the probate court for an order requiring the executor or administrator to distribute the assets of the estate, either in whole or in part, in cash or in kind. Upon notice to the executor or administrator, the court shall inquire into the condition of the estate, and if all claims have been paid, or adequate provision has been or can be made for their payment, the court shall make such order with reference to distribution of the estate as the condition of the estate and the protection of all parties interested in the estate may demand. The order of the court shall provide that assets be set aside for the payment of claims rejected within two months or in suit, and each claimant for whom assets are to be set aside shall be entitled to be fully heard as to the nature and amount of the assets to be set aside for payment of his claim, and as to all other conditions in connection with the

claim. Each legatee or distributee receiving distribution from the estate shall be liable to return the assets distributed to him, or the proceeds from the assets, if they are necessary to pay such claims. The court, upon its own motion or upon application of the executor or administrator, as a condition precedent to any distribution, may require any legatee or distributee to give bond to the state with surety approved and in an amount fixed by the court, conditioned as provided in section 2113.53 of the Revised Code or as may be directed by the court. Such bond may be in addition to the assets to be set aside or partially or wholly in lieu of those assets, as the court shall determine.

HISTORY: GC § 10509-182; 114 v 320 (441); 119 v 394 (415); Bureau of Code Revision, 10-1-53; 125 v 903 (977) (Eff 10-1-53); 133 v S 185 (Eff 1-1-71); 136 v S 145 (Eff 1-1-76); 143 v H 346. Eff 5-31-90.

§ 2113.55 Distribution in kind.

Before making distribution in kind of property which is not specifically bequeathed, an executor or administrator shall obtain the approval of the probate court or the consent of all of the legatees or distributees whose interests may be affected by such distribution. A distribution in kind may be made to any beneficiary, including an executor, administrator, trustee, guardian, and the surviving spouse.

HISTORY: GC § 10509-183; 114 v 320(441); 119 v 394(416); Bureau of Code Revision. Eff 10-1-53.

§ 2113.56 Executor or administrator not liable.

An executor or administrator is not liable for any distribution made in compliance with sections 2113.53, 2113.54, and 2113.55 of the Revised Code, except that an order of distribution made pursuant to any of such sections may be vacated as provided in section 2109.35 of the Revised Code relating to accounts.

HISTORY: GC § 10509-183a; 119 v 394(424), § 8; 121 v 270; Bureau of Code Revision. Eff 10-1-53.

§ 2113.57 Distribution after settlement.

If upon hearing and settlement of an executor's or administrator's account, a balance due the estate remains in the hands of the executor or administrator, the court may order distribution to be made by him.

HISTORY: GC § 10509-184; 114 v 320(441); Bureau of Code Revision. Eff 10-1-53.

§ 2113.58 Protection of remainderman's interest in personal property.

When by a last will and testament the use or income of personal property is given to a person for a term of years or for life and some other person has an interest in such property as remainderman, the probate court, unless such last will and testament otherwise provides, may deliver such personal property to the person having the limited estate, with or without bond, as the court may determine; or the court may order that such property be held by the executor or some other trustee, with or without bond, for the benefit of the person having the limited estate. If bond is required of the person having the limited estate, or of the trustee, it may be increased or decreased, and if bond is not required in the first instance it may be required by the court at any time prior to the termination of the limited estate.

HISTORY: GC § 10509-185; 114 v 320(442); Bureau of Code Revision. Eff 10-1-53.

§ 2113.59 Lien on share of beneficiary.

When a beneficiary of an estate is indebted to such estate, the amount of the indebtedness if due, or the present worth of the indebtedness if not due, may be set off by the executor or administrator against any testate or intestate share of the estate to which such beneficiary is entitled.

HISTORY: GC § 10509-186; 114 v 320(442); Bureau of Code Revision. Eff 10-1-53.

§ 2113.85 Definitions.

As used in sections 2113.85 to 2113.90 of the Revised Code:

(A) "Estate" means the gross estate of a decedent who is domiciled in this state, as determined for federal estate tax purposes under Subtitle B of the "Internal Revenue Code of 1954," 26 U.S.C. 2001, as amended, for Ohio estate tax purposes under Chapter 5731. of the Revised Code, and for estate tax purposes of any other jurisdiction that imposes a tax on the transfer of property by a decedent who is domiciled in this state.

(B) "Person interested in the estate" means any person who is entitled to receive, or who has received, any property or property interest included in the decedent's estate. A "person interested in the estate" includes, but is not limited to, a personal representative, guardian, and trustee. A "person interested in the estate" does not include a creditor of the decedent or of his estate.

(C) "Tax" means the federal estate tax determined under Subtitle B of the "Internal Revenue Code of 1954," 26 U.S.C. 2001, as amended, an Ohio estate tax determined under Chapter 5731. of the Revised Code, and the estate tax determined by any other jurisdiction that imposes a tax on the transfer of property by a decedent who is domiciled in this state.

(D) "Fiduciary" means an executor, administrator, or other person who, by virtue of his representation of the decedent's estate, is required to pay the tax.

HISTORY: 138 v S 317 (Eff 3-23-81); 141 v H 139. Eff 7-24-86.

§ 2113.86 Apportionment of taxes.

(A) Unless a will or another governing instrument otherwise provides, and except as otherwise provided in this section, a tax shall be apportioned equitably in accordance with the provisions of this section among all persons interested in an estate in proportion to the value of the interest of each person as determined for estate tax purposes.

(B) Except as otherwise provided in this division, any tax that is apportioned against a gift made in a clause of a will other than a residuary clause or in a provision of an inter vivos trust other than a residuary provision, shall be reapportioned to the residue of the estate or trust. It shall be charged in the same manner as a general administration expense. However, when a portion of the residue of the estate or trust is allowable as a deduction for estate tax purposes, the tax shall be reapportioned to the extent possible to the portion of the residue that is not so allowable.

(C)(1) A tax shall not be apportioned against an interest that is allowable as an estate tax marital or charitable deduction, except to the extent that the interest is a part of the residue of an estate or trust against which tax is reapportioned pursuant to division (B) of this section.

(2) Estate tax of this state or another jurisdiction shall not be reapportioned against an interest that is allowable as a deduction for federal estate tax purposes, to the extent that there is other property in the estate or trust that is not allowable as a deduction for federal estate tax purposes and against which estate tax of this state or another jurisdiction can be apportioned.

(D) A tax shall not be apportioned against property that passes to a surviving spouse as an elective share under section 2106.01 of the Revised Code or as an intestate share under section 2105.06 of the Revised Code, to the extent that there is other property in the estate that is not allowable as a deduction for estate tax purposes against which the tax can be apportioned.

(E)(1) Any federal estate tax credit for state or foreign death taxes on property that is includible in an estate for federal estate tax purposes, shall inure to the benefit of the persons chargeable with the payment of the state or foreign death taxes in proportion to the amount of the taxes paid by each person, but any federal estate tax credit for state or foreign death taxes inuring to the benefit of a person cannot exceed the federal estate tax apportioned to that person.

(2) Any federal estate tax credit for gift taxes paid by a donee of a gift shall inure to the benefit of that donee for purposes of this section.

(3) Credits against tax not covered by division (E)(1) or (2) of this section shall be apportioned equitably among persons in the manner in which the tax is apportioned among them.

(F) Any additional estate tax that is due because a qualified heir has disposed of qualified farm property in a manner not authorized by law or ceased to use any part of the qualified farm property for a qualified use, shall be apportioned against the interest of the qualified heir.

(G) If both a present interest and a future interest in property are involved, a tax shall be apportioned entirely to the principal. This shall be the case even if the future interest qualifies for an estate tax charitable deduction, even if the holder of the present interest also has rights in the principal, and even if the principal is otherwise exempt from apportionment.

(H) Penalties shall be apportioned in the same manner as a tax, and interest on tax shall be apportioned to the income of the estate or trust, unless a court directs a different apportionment of penalties or interest based on a finding that special circumstances make an apportionment as provided in this division inequitable.

(I) If any part of an estate consists of property, the value of which is included in the gross estate of the decedent by reason of section 2044 of the "Internal Revenue Code of 1986," 100 Stat. 2085, 26 U.S.C.A. 2044, as amended, or of section 5731.131 [5731.13.1] of the Revised Code, the estate is entitled to recover from the persons holding or receiving the property any amount by which the estate tax payable exceeds the estate tax that would have been payable if the value of the property had not been included in the gross estate of the decedent. This division does not apply if a decedent provides otherwise in his will or another governing instrument and the will or instrument refers to either section mentioned in this division or to qualified terminable interest marital deduction property.

HISTORY: 141 v H 139 (Eff 7-24-86); 143 v H 346. Eff 5-31-90.

§ 2115.01 "Inventory" defined.

As used in Chapters 2113. to 2125., inclusive, of the Revised Code, "inventory" includes appraisement.

HISTORY: GC § 10509-40; 114 v 320(411); Bureau of Code Revision. Eff 10-1-53.

§ 2115.02 Inventory; separate schedule.

Within one month after the date of his appointment, unless the probate court grants an extension of time for good cause shown, every executor or administrator shall make and return on oath into court a true inventory of the real estate of the decedent located in this state, and the chattels, moneys, rights, and credits of the decedent that are to be administered and that have come to his possession or knowledge. The inventory is to be based on values as of the date of death of the decedent. If his predecessors have done so, a fiduciary need not return and file an inventory, unless, in the opinion of the court, it is necessary.

Any assets, the value of which is readily ascertainable without the exercise of judgment on the part of an appraiser, shall not be appraised. The value of these assets shall be shown in the inventory and verified by the administrator or executor, and he shall provide evidence of value as the court requires.

HISTORY: GC § 10509-41; 114 v 320(411); 116 v 385; Bureau of Code Revision, 10-1-53; 133 v S 185 (Eff 1-1-71); 136 v S 145 (Eff 1-1-76); 142 v S 228. Eff 3-22-89.

§ 2115.03 Proceedings on refusal to file inventory.

If an executor or administrator neglects or refuses to return an inventory as provided by section 2115.02 of the Revised Code, the probate court shall issue an order requiring him, at an early day therein named, to return an inventory.

After personal service of such order by a person authorized to make the service, if such executor or administrator, by the day appointed, does not return such inventory under oath or fails to obtain further time from the court to return it, or if such order cannot be served personally by reason of his absconding or concealing himself, the court may remove such executor or administrator and new letters shall be granted.

Such letters shall supersede all former letters testamentary or of administration, deprive the former executor or administrator of all power, authority, or control over the estate of the deceased, and entitle the person appointed to take, demand, and receive the effects of such deceased wherever they are found.

In every case of the revocation of such letters, the bond given by the former executor or administrator must be prosecuted and a recovery had thereon to the full extent of any injury sustained by the estate of the deceased, by such executor's or administrator's acts or omissions, and to the full value of all property of the deceased, received and not administered by him.

HISTORY: GC §§ 10509-62—10509-65; 114 v 320(415, 416); Bureau of Code Revision. Eff 10-1-53.

§ 2115.04 Notice of inventory.

Not less than five days previous

thereto, a written notice stating the time and place of making the inventory required by section 2115.02 of the Revised Code, must be served by the executor or administrator on the surviving spouse, but such notice may be waived in writing by such surviving spouse.

HISTORY: GC § 10509-45; 114 v 320(412); Bureau of Code Revision. Eff 10-1-53.

§ 2115.05 Who shall make inventory.

After giving the notice required in section 2115.04 of the Revised Code, the executor or administrator, with the aid of the appraiser, if an appraisement is to be made, shall make the inventory required by section 2115.02 of the Revised Code.

HISTORY: GC § 10509-44; 114 v 320(412); Bureau of Code Revision, 10-1-53; 133 v S 185. Eff 1-1-71.

The effective date is set by § 3 of the act.

SECTION 3. (133 v S 185) §§ 1 and 2 of this act shall take effect on January 1, 1971. This act does not affect the administration of the estates of persons who die before January 1, 1971, and the estates of such persons shall be administered as if this act had not been passed and approved.

§ 2115.06 Appraisers; compensation; fees may be charged against the estate.

The real estate and personal property comprised in the inventory required by section 2115.02 of the Revised Code, unless an appraisement thereof has been dispensed with by an order of the probate court, shall be appraised by one suitable disinterested person appointed by the executor or administrator, subject to the approval of the court and sworn to a faithful discharge of his trust. The executor or administrator, subject to the approval of the court, may appoint separate appraisers of property located in any other county and appoint separate appraisers for each asset.

If appraisers fail to attend to the performance of their duty, the executor or administrator, subject to the approval of the probate judge may appoint others to supply the place of such delinquents.

Each appraiser shall be paid such amount for his services as determined by the executor or administrator, subject to the approval of the probate judge, taking into consideration his training, qualifications, experience, time reasonably required, and the value of the property appraised. The amount of such fees may be charged against the estate as part of the cost of the proceeding.

HISTORY: GC §§ 10509-42, 10509-43, 10509-58; 114 v 320(415); Bureau of Code Revision, 10-1-53; 125 v 52 (Eff 10-2-53); 133 v S 185 (Eff 1-1-71); 136 v S 145 (Eff 1-1-76); 136 v S 466. Eff 5-26-76.

§ 2115.07 Oath and duties of appraisers.

Before proceeding to the execution of their duty, the appraisers of a decedent's estate must take and subscribe to an oath, to be inserted in or annexed to the inventory required by section 2115.02 of the Revised Code, before an officer authorized to administer oaths, that they will truly, honestly, and impartially appraise the estate and property exhibited to them, and perform the other duties required in the premises according to the best of their knowledge and ability. In the absence of such officer, the administrator or executor may administer the oath.

In the presence of the surviving spouse, next of kin, legatees, or creditors of the testator or intestate, or such of them as attend, the appraisers shall proceed to estimate and appraise the property and estate. Each item must be set down separately, with its value in dollars and cents in distinct figures opposite such item.

HISTORY: GC §§ 10509-46, 10509-47; 114 v 320(412); Bureau of Code Revision. Eff 10-1-53.

§ 2115.08 Repealed, 133 v S 185, § 2 [GC § 10509-48; 114 v 320(413); Bureau of Code Revision, 10-1-53]. Eff 1-1-71.

This section concerned household goods.

§ 2115.09 Inventory contents.

The inventory required by section 2115.02 of the Revised Code shall contain a particular statement of all securities for the payment of money which belong to the deceased and are known to such executor or administrator. Such inventory shall specify the name of the debtor in each security, the date, the sum originally payable, the indorsements thereon with their dates, the serial numbers or other identifying data as to each security, and the sum which, in the judgment of the appraisers, can be collected on each claim.

Such inventory must contain a statement of all debts and accounts belonging to the deceased which are known to such executor or administrator and specify the name of the debtor, the date, the balance or thing due, and the value or sum which can be collected thereon, in the judgment of the appraisers.

Such inventory must contain an account of all moneys which belong to the deceased and have come to the hands of the executor or administrator. If none has come to his hands, the fact must be stated in the inventory.

HISTORY: GC §§ 10509-51—10509-53; 114 v 320(413); Bureau of Code Revision. Eff 10-1-53.

§ 2115.10 Emblements are assets.

The emblements raised by labor, whether severed or not from the land of the deceased at the time of his death, are assets in the hands of the executor or administrator and shall be included in the inventory required by section 2115.02 of the Revised Code.

The executor or administrator, or the person to whom he sells such emblements, at all reasonable times may enter upon the lands to cultivate, sever, and gather them.

HISTORY: GC §§ 10509-49, 10509-50; 114 v 320(413); Bureau of Code Revision. Eff 10-1-53.

§ 2115.11 Discharge of a debt in a will.

The discharge, or bequest, in a will, of a debt or demand of a testator against an executor named therein, or against any other person, is not valid as against the decedent's creditors, but is only a specific bequest of such debt or demand. The amount thereof must be included in the inventory of the credits and effects of the deceased and, if necessary, such amount must be applied in the payment of his debts. If not necessary for that purpose, such amount shall be paid in the same manner and proportion as other specific legacies.

HISTORY: GC § 10509-66; 114 v 320(416); Bureau of Code Revision. Eff 10-1-53.

§ 2115.12 Naming of person as executor does not discharge debt.

The naming of a person as executor in a will shall not operate as a discharge or bequest of a just claim which the testator had against such executor. Such claim shall be included among the assets of the deceased in the inventory required by section 2115.02 of the Revised Code. The executor shall be liable for it as for so much money in his hands at the time such debt or demand becomes due, and must apply and distribute it as part of the personal estate of the deceased.

HISTORY: GC § 10509-67; 114 v 320(416); 116 v PtII 255; 119 v 394(405); Bureau of Code Revision. Eff 10-1-53.

§ 2115.13 Repealed, 136 v S 145, § 2 [GC §§ 10509-54, 10509-55; 114 v 320; 119 v 394; Bureau of Code Revision, 10-1-53; 125 v 903] Eff 1-1-76.

This section concerned property exempt from administration.

§ 2115.14 Repealed, 136 v S 145, § 2 [GC § 10509-76; 114 v 320; Bureau of Code Revision, 10-1-53]. Eff 1-1-76.

This section concerned allowance stated in separate schedule.

§ 2115.15 Signing, certifying, and return of inventory.

Upon the completion of the inventory required by section 2115.02 of the Revised Code, such inventory shall be signed by the appraisers at the end thereof and said appraisers shall certify that the inventory is a true and correct appraisement of the property exhibited to them. It is not necessary for the appraisers to sign each schedule thereof. A copy of the inventory shall be retained by the executor or administrator who shall return the original to the probate court.

Before such inventory is received by the court, the executor or administrator shall take and subscribe to an oath or affirmation before an officer authorized to administer oaths stating that the inventory is in all respects just and true and that it contains a true statement of all the estate and property of the deceased which has come to his knowledge, particularly of all money belonging to the deceased, and of all just claims of the deceased against such executor or administrator, or other persons, according to the best of his knowledge. Such oath must be indorsed upon or annexed to the inventory.

HISTORY: GC §§ 10509-56, 10509-57; 114 v 320(414); Bureau of Code Revision. Eff 10-1-53.

§ 2115.16 Hearing on inventory.

Upon the filing of the inventory required by section 2115.02 of the Revised Code, the probate court shall forthwith set a day, not later than one month after the day the inventory was filed, for a hearing on the inventory and shall give at least ten days' notice by certified mail or otherwise of the hearing to the executor or administrator and to each of the following whose place of residence is known:

(A) Surviving spouse;

(B) Next of kin;

(C) Beneficiaries under the will;

(D) The attorneys, if known, representing any of the persons described in divisions (A) to (C) of this section.

Such notice may be waived in writing by any of the persons described in divisions (A) to (D) of this section. For good cause, the hearing may be continued for such time as the court considers reasonable. Exceptions to the inventory or to the allowance for support provided by section 2106.13 of the Revised Code may be filed at any time prior to five days before the date set for the hearing or the date to which the hearing has been continued, by any person interested in the estate or in any of the property included in the inventory, but the time limit for the filing of exceptions shall not apply in case of fraud or concealment of assets. When exceptions are filed, notice of them and the time of the hearing on them shall forthwith be given to the executor or administrator and his attorney by certified mail or by personal service, unless the notice is waived. At the hearing, the executor or administrator and any witness may be examined under oath. The court shall enter its finding on the journal and tax the costs as may be equitable.

HISTORY: GC § 10509-59; 114 v 320 (415); 116 v 385; Bureau of Code Revision, 10-1-53; 125 v 903 (978); 126 v 392 (Eff 3-17-55); 143 v H 346. Eff 5-31-90.

§ 2115.17 Real estate appraisal conclusive.

When the inventory required by section 2115.02 of the Revised Code has been approved by the probate court, the appraisement of the real estate as set forth therein shall be conclusive for all purposes except estate tax, unless a reappraisal is ordered by the court.

HISTORY: GC § 10509-61; 114 v 320(415); Bureau of Code Revision, 10-1-53; 132 v S 326, § 1. Eff 7-1-68.

§ 2127.01 Sale of lands by executors and administrators.

All proceedings for the sale of lands by executors, administrators, and guardians shall be in accordance with section[s] 2127.01 to 2127.43, inclusive, of the Revised Code, except where the executor has testamentary power of sale, and in that case the executor may proceed under such sections or under the will.

HISTORY: GC § 10510-1; 114 v 320(451); 119 v 394(418); Bureau of Code Revision. Eff 10-1-53.

§ 3107.15 Effect of adoption.

(A) A final decree of adoption and an interlocutory order of adoption that has become final, issued by a court of this state, shall have the following effects as to all matters within the jurisdiction or before a court of this state:

(1) Except with respect to a spouse of the petitioner and relatives of the spouse, to relieve the biological or other legal parents of the adopted person of all parental rights and responsibilities, and to terminate all legal relationships between the adopted person and his relatives, including his biological or other legal parents, so that the adopted person thereafter is a stranger to his former relatives for all purposes including inheritance and the interpretation or construction of documents, statutes, and instruments, whether executed before or after the adoption is decreed, which do not expressly include the person by name or by some designation not based on a parent and child or blood relationship;

(2) To create the relationship of parent and child between petitioner and the adopted person, as if the adopted person were a legitimate blood descendant of the petitioner, for all purposes including inheritance and applicability of statutes, documents, and instruments, whether executed before or after the adoption is decreed, which do not ex- pressly exclude an adopted person from their operation or effect.

(B) Notwithstanding division (A) of this section, if a parent of a child dies without the relationship of parent and child having been previously terminated and a spouse of the living parent thereafter adopts the child, the child's rights from or through the deceased parent for all purposes, including inheritance and applicability or construction of documents, statutes, and instruments, are not restricted or curtailed by the adoption.

(C) An interlocutory order of adoption, while it is in force, has the same legal effect as a final decree of adoption. If an interlocutory order of adoption is vacated, it shall be as though void from its issuance, and the rights, liabilities, and status of all affected persons that have not become vested are governed accordingly.

HISTORY: 136 v H 156. Eff 1-1-77.

§ 5731.01 Definitions.

As used in this chapter:

(A) The "value of the gross estate" of the decedent shall include, to the extent provided in sections 5731.03 to 5731.131 [5731.13.1] of the Revised Code, the value, on the date of the decedent's death or on an alternate valuation date prescribed by division (D) of this section, of all property, real or personal, tangible or intangible, wherever situated, except real property situated and tangible personal property having an actual situs outside of this state.

(B) Subject to the provisions of section 5731.011 [5731.01.1] of the Revised Code that permit a valuation of qualified farm property at its value for its actual qualified use, the value of any property included in the gross estate shall be the price at which such property would change hands between a willing buyer and a willing seller, neither being under any compulsion to buy or sell and both having reasonable knowledge of relevant facts. All relevant facts and elements of value as of the valuation date shall be considered in determining such value.

The rulings and regulations of the internal revenue service and decisions of the federal courts defining the principles applicable in determining fair market value for purposes of the federal estate tax imposed by Subchapter A, Chapter 11 of the Internal Revenue Code of 1954, 26 U.S.C. 2001, as amended, shall be applied in determining fair market value for purposes of the estate taxes imposed by this chapter, to the extent that these rulings, regulations, and decisions are not inconsistent with the express provisions of this chapter, but the actual determination of the fair market value by the internal revenue service of any asset included in the gross estate is not controlling for purposes of the estate taxes imposed by this chapter unless the person filing the estate tax return and the tax commissioner have agreed in writing to be bound by the federal determination, as provided in section 5731.26 of the Revised Code.

(C) In the case of stock and securities of a corporation the value of which, by reason of their not being listed on an exchange and by reason of the absence of sales of them, cannot be determined with reference to bid and asked prices, or with reference to sales prices, the value of them shall be determined by taking into consideration, in addition to all other factors, the value of stock or securities of corporations engaged in the same or a similar line of business which are listed on an exchange or which are traded actively in the over-the-counter market.

If a valuation of securities is undertaken by reference to market transactions and if the block of securities to be valued is so large in relation to actual sales on existing markets that it could not be liquidated in a reasonable time without depressing the market, the price at which the block could be sold, as such, outside the usual market, as through an underwriter, shall be considered in determining the value of such block of securities.

(D) "Alternate valuation date" means the date for valuation of a gross estate permitted by filing an election under this division. Whether or not an alternate valuation date election is available to an estate for federal estate tax purposes or, if available, is made for the estate, the value of the gross estate may be determined, if the person required to file the estate tax return so elects, by valuing all the property included in the gross estate on the alternate date, if any, provided in section 2032 (a) of the Internal Revenue Code of 1954, 26 U.S.C. 2032(a), as amended as such section generally applies, for federal estate tax purposes, to the estates of persons dying on the decedent's date of death.

No deduction under this chapter of any item shall be allowed if allowance is, in effect, given by use of the alternate valuation date. In the determination of any tax liability of any estate in which an election is filed under this division, all provisions in this chapter which refer to value at the time of the decedent's death shall be construed for all purposes to mean the value of such property used in determining the value of the gross estate. For the purposes of the charitable deduction under section 5731.17 of the Revised Code, any bequest, legacy, devise, or transfer enumerated in it shall be valued as of the date of the decedent's death with adjustment for any difference in value, not due to mere lapse of time or the occurrence or nonoccurrence of a contingency, of the property as of the date six months after the decedent's death, or in case of its earlier disposition, on such date of disposition.

An election under this division shall be exercised on the estate tax return by the person required to file the return. When made, an election under this division is irrevocable. An election cannot be exercised under this division if a return is filed more than one year after the time prescribed, including any extensions of time granted, pursuant to law for filing the return.

(E) Unless otherwise indicated by the context, "county" means one of the following:

(1) The county in which the decedent's estate is administered;

(2) If no administration of the decedent's estate is being had, the county of residence of the decedent at the time of his death;

(3) If the decedent dies a resident of another state, any county in which any property subject to tax is located.

HISTORY: 132 v S 326 (Eff 7-1-68); 134 v S 398 (Eff 4-1-72); 139 v S 28 (Eff 10-9-81); 140 v H 291 (Eff 7-1-83); 141 v H 139. Eff 7-24-86.

The provisions of § 3 of HB 139 (141 v —) read as follows:

SECTION 3. Except as provided in Sections 4, 5, and 6 of this act and except for sections 1339.66 and 2109.62 of the Revised Code as enacted by this act, Sections 1 and 2 of this act shall apply only to the estates of decedents whose death occurs on or after the effective date of this act.

The provisions of § 127 of HB 291 (140 v —) read as follows:

SECTION 127. The amendment of sections 2117.06, 5731.01, 5731.011, 5731.02, 5731.05, 5731.09, 5731.14, 5731.15, 5731.16, 5731.18, 5731.21, 5731.22, 5731.26, 5731.42, and 5731.48, the enactment of sections 5731.131, 5731.181, 5731.231, and 5731.99, and the repeal of section 5731.20 of the Revised Code, all by this act, shall apply to the estate of any decedent whose death occurs on or after July 1, 1983.

[§ 5731.01.1] § 5731.011
Valuation of a qualified farm property; recapture tax upon early disposition.

(A) As used in this section:

(1) "Adjusted value" means:

(a) In the case of the gross estate, the value of the gross estate as determined pursuant to section 5731.01 of the Revised Code and without regard to this section, reduced by any amounts allowable as a deduction under division (A)(4) of section 5731.16 of the Revised Code;

(b) In the case of any real or personal property, the value of the property as determined pursuant to section 5731.01 of the Revised Code and without regard to this section, reduced by any amounts allowable as a deduction in respect to such property under division (A)(4) of section 5731.16 of the Revised Code.

(2) "Member of the decedent's family" means, with respect to any decedent, only his ancestor or lineal descendant, a lineal descendant of any of his grandparents, his spouse, the spouse of any such descendant, or a step child or foster child of the decedent.

(3) "Qualified farm property" means real property that is located in this state, that is included in the gross estate of the decedent under this chapter, and that was acquired by, or passed to, a qualified heir, but only if both of the following apply:

(a) Fifty per cent or more of the adjusted value of the gross estate consists of the adjusted value of real or personal property which, on the date of the decedent's death, was being used for a qualified use;

(b) Twenty-five per cent or more of the adjusted value of the gross estate consists of the adjusted value of real property which, on the date of the decedent's death, was being used for a qualified use.

(4) "Qualified heir" means a member of the decedent's family who acquired qualified farm property, or to whom such property passed. If a qualified heir disposes of any interest in qualified farm property to any member of the decedent's family, that member shall thereafter be treated as the qualified heir with respect to the interest.

(5) "Qualified use" means the devotion of real property exclusively to agricultural use as described in the definition of "land devoted exclusively to agricultural use" contained in division (A) of section 5713.30 of the Revised Code, whether or not an application has been filed by the decedent or a qualified heir

pursuant to section 5713.31 of the Revised Code.

(B)(1) For purposes of determining the value of property included in the gross estate, the value of qualified farm property is, subject to division (D) of this section, whichever of the following the person filing the estate tax return elects:

(a) Its fair market value, as determined pursuant to division (B) of section 5731.01 of the Revised Code;

(b) Its value for its actual qualified use, on the date of the decedent's death or on an alternate valuation date prescribed by division (D) of section 5731.01 of the Revised Code;

(c) Its value for its actual qualified use, as determined under section 5713.31 of the Revised Code.

(2) The election shall be made on or before the date by which the return is required to be filed, determined with regard to any extension of time granted pursuant to law for filing the return.

(C)(1) For purposes of this section, the existence of a qualified use may be established, but is not required to be established, by the filing of an application pursuant to section 5713.31 of the Revised Code and its approval by the county auditor.

(2) This section applies to any interest in qualified farm property that is held in a partnership, corporation, or trust, if the interest would qualify under this section if it were held directly by the decedent.

(D) If the person filing the estate tax return elects pursuant to division (B)(1)(b) or (c) of this section, to have qualified farm property valued at its value for its actual qualified use, and if the difference between the fair market value of the property as determined pursuant to division (B) of section 5731.01 of the Revised Code and the value for its actual qualified use under division (B)(1)(b) or (c) of this section, whichever was elected, exceeds five hundred thousand dollars, the property shall be valued at the amount that is five hundred thousand dollars less than the fair market value.

(E) If an election is made, pursuant to division (B)(1)(b) or (c) of this section, to have qualified farm property valued at its value for its actual qualified use, and if, within four years after the date of the decedent's death and before the death of the qualified heir, the qualified heir disposes of any interest in the property to a person other than a member of the decedent's family, or ceases to use any part of the property for a qualified use, a recapture tax shall be imposed. The recapture tax shall be equivalent to the estate tax savings realized in the decedent's estate by valuating the interest disposed of, or the part of the property that has ceased to be used for a qualified use, at its value for its actual qualified use, instead of at its fair market value pursuant to division (B) of section 5731.01 of the Revised Code. The recapture tax, plus interest computed at the rate per annum determined under section 5703.47 of the Revised Code, from nine months after the date of the decedent's death, is due and payable on the day that is nine months after the date of the disposition or cessation of use, and shall be paid by the qualified heir who disposed of the interest or ceased use of the part of the property for a qualified use.

(F) The tax commissioner shall prescribe rules and forms to implement this section. The rules may require, for purposes of division (E) of this section, that a qualified heir file an annual report with the commissioner, establishing that the qualified farm property has not been disposed of to a person other than a member of the decedent's family and that no part of it has ceased to be used for a qualified use.

HISTORY: 139 v S 28 (Eff 10-9-81); 140 v H 291 (Eff 7-1-83); 141 v H 139. Eff 7-24-86.

See provisions, § 3 of HB 139 (141 v —) following RC § 5731.01.

See provisions, § 127 of HB 291 (140 v —) following RC § 5731.01.

§ 5731.02 Estate tax; rates.

(A) A tax is hereby levied on the transfer of the taxable estate, determined as provided in section 5731.14 of the Revised Code, of every person dying on or after July 1, 1968, who at the time of his death was a resident of this state, as follows:

If the taxable estate is:	The tax shall be:
Not over $40,000	2% of the taxable estate
Over $40,000 but not over $100,000	$800 plus 3% of the excess over $40,000
Over $100,000 but not over $200,000	$2,600 plus 4% of the excess over $100,000
Over $200,000 but not over $300,000	$6,600 plus 5% of the excess over $200,000
Over $300,000 but not over $500,000	$11,600 plus 6% of the excess over $300,000
Over $500,000	$23,600 plus 7% of the excess over $500,000.

(B) A credit shall be allowed against the tax imposed by division (A) of this section equal to the lesser of five hundred dollars or the amount of the tax.

HISTORY: 132 v S 326 (Eff 7-1-68); 140 v H 291. Eff 7-1-83.

See provisions, § 127 of HB 291 (140 v —) following RC § 5731.01.

§ 5731.03 Interest of decedent.

The value of the gross estate shall include the value of all property, to the extent of the interest therein of the decedent on the date of the decedent's death.

HISTORY: 132 v S 326. Eff 7-1-68.

§ 5731.04 Interest of surviving spouse.

The value of the gross estate shall include the value of all property, to the extent of any interest therein of the surviving spouse, existing on the date of the decedent's death as dower or curtesy or by virtue of a statute creating an estate in lieu of dower or curtesy.

HISTORY: 132 v S 326. Eff 7-1-68.

§ 5731.05 Transfers in contemplation of death.

Note: See following version effective 7-1-93.

(A) Except as provided in divisions (B) and (C) of this section, the value of the gross estate shall include the value of all property, to the extent of any interest in property, of which the decedent has at any time made a transfer, by trust or otherwise, in contemplation of his death.

(B) Any transfer, except as provided in division (C) of this section, by trust or otherwise, made within a period of three years ending with the date of the decedent's death shall be deemed to have been made in contemplation of death, unless the contrary is shown. No transfer made before that three-year period shall be treated as having been made in contemplation of death.

(C) This section does not apply to any of the following:

(1) A bona fide sale for an adequate and full consideration in money or money's worth;

(2) A transfer of property that would not be included in the decedent's gross estate if retained by him until death;

(3) The first ten thousand dollars of the transfers that were made by the decedent to each transferee in each calendar year, but only to the extent that those transfers qualify as present interests under section 2503(b) and (c) of the "Internal Revenue Code of 1986," 26 U.S.C. 2503, as amended. The exclusion provided by division (C)(3) of this section does not apply to any portion of a transfer that is treated as being made by the spouse of the decedent under section 2513 of the "Internal Revenue Code of 1986," 26 U.S.C. 2513, as amended.

(4) Federal or state gift taxes paid with respect to any includible transfer.

(D) The amendments made to this section by Substitute Senate Bill No. 336 of the 118th general assembly shall apply only to the estates of decedents who die on or after the effective date of those amendments.

HISTORY: 132 v S 326 (Eff 7-1-68); 140 v H 291 (Eff 7-1-83); 140 v H 794 (Eff 7-6-84); 141 v H 139 (Eff 7-24-86); 143 v H 111, § 1 (Eff 7-1-89); 143 v S 336, § 1. Eff 4-10-90.

The provisions of §§ 3–5 of SB 336 (143 v —) read as follows:

SECTION 3. That the versions of sections 5731.05, 5731.131, and 5731.15 of the Revised Code that are to be effective July 1, 1993, be amended to read as follows:

§ 5731.05 Transfers in contemplation of death.

Note: See preceding version in effect until 7-1-93.

(A) Except as provided in divisions (B) and (C) of this section, the value of the gross estate shall include the value of all property, to the extent of any interest in property, of which the decedent has at any time made a transfer, by trust or otherwise, in contemplation of his death.

(B) Any transfer, except as provided in division (C) of this section, by trust or otherwise, made within a period of three years ending with the date of the decedent's death shall be deemed to have been made in contemplation of death, unless the contrary is shown. No transfer made before that three-year period shall be treated as having been made in contemplation of death.

(C) This section does not apply to any of the following:

(1) A bona fide sale for an adequate and full consideration in money or money's worth;

(2) A transfer of property that would not be included in the decedent's gross estate if retained by him until death;

(3) The first ten thousand dollars of the transfers that were made by the decedent to each transferee, other than the spouse of the decedent, in each calendar year, but only to the extent that those transfers qualify as present interests under section 2503(b) and (c) of the "Internal Revenue Code of 1986," 26 U.S.C. 2503, as amended. The exclusion provided by division (C)(3) of this section does not apply to any portion of a transfer that is treated as being made by the spouse of the decedent under section 2513 of the "Internal Revenue Code of 1986," 26 U.S.C. 2513, as amended.

(4) A transfer of property made to the spouse of the transferor, except as provided in section 5731.131 [5731.13.1] of the Revised Code;

(5) Federal or state gift taxes paid with respect to any includible transfer.

(D) The amendments made to this section by Amended Substitute House Bill No. 111 and substitute Senate Bill No. 336 of the 118th general assembly that are effective on July 1, 1993, shall apply only to the estates of decedents who die on or after that date.

*HISTORY: . . . . 143 v H 111, § 3 (Eff 7-1-93); 143 v S 336, § 3. Eff 7-1-93.

SECTION 4. That all existing versions of sections 5731.05, 5731.131, and 5731.15 of the Revised Code are hereby repealed.

SECTION 5. Sections 3 and 4 of this act shall take effect on July 1, 1993.

See provisions, § 3 of HB 139 (141 v —) following RC § 5731.01.

See provisions, § 127 of HB 291 (140 v —) following RC § 5731.01.

§ 5731.06 Transfers with retention of life estate or power of appointment.

The value of the gross estate shall include the value of all property, to the extent of any interest therein of which the decedent has at any time made a transfer, except in the case of a bona fide sale for an adequate and full consideration in money or money's worth, by trust or otherwise, under which he has retained for his life or for any period not ascertainable without reference to his death or for any period which does not in fact end before his death the possession or enjoyment of, or the right to the income from, the property, or the right, either alone or in conjunction with any person, to designate the persons who shall possess or enjoy the property or the income therefrom.

HISTORY: 132 v S 326. Eff 7-1-68.

§ 5731.07 Transfers conditioned on survivorship, reversionary interest.

(A) The value of the gross estate shall include the value of all property, to the extent of any interest therein of which the decedent has at any time made a transfer, except in the case of a bona fide sale for an adequate and full consideration in money or money's worth, by trust or otherwise, if both of the following conditions exist:

(1) Possession or enjoyment of the property can, through ownership of such interest, be obtained only by surviving the decedent; and

(2) The decedent has retained a reversionary interest by the express terms of the instrument of transfer and the value of such reversionary interest immediately before the death of the decedent exceeds five per cent of the value of such property.

(B) "Reversionary interest" includes a possibility that property transferred by the decedent may return to him or to his estate or become subject to a power of disposition by him and its value shall be determined immediately before the death of the decedent by the usual methods of valuation, including the use of tables of mortality and actuarial principles, under rules and regulations prescribed by the tax commissioner.

HISTORY: 132 v S 326. Eff 7-1-68.

§ **5731.08** Transfers subject to power to alter, amend, revoke, or terminate.

The value of the gross estate shall include the value of all property, to the extent of any interest therein of which the decedent has made a transfer except in the case of a bona fide sale for an adequate and full consideration in money or money's worth, by trust or otherwise, where the enjoyment thereof was subject on the date of the decedent's death to any change through the exercise of a power, in whatever capacity exercisable, by the decedent alone or by the decedent in conjunction with any other person to alter, amend, revoke or terminate.

HISTORY: 132 v S 326. Eff 7-1-68.

§ **5731.09** Annuities; employer death benefit plan.

(A) The value of the gross estate shall include the value of an annuity or other payment receivable by a beneficiary by reason of surviving the decedent under any form of contract or agreement, including the value of an annuity or other payment receivable by any beneficiary under any form of contract or agreement as is proportionate to the purchase price contributed by an employer or former employer which is excludable from the gross estate by reason of subchapter A, Chapter 11, subtitle B, of the Internal Revenue Code of 1954, 26 U.S.C. 2039 if, under such contract or agreement, an annuity or similar payment was payable to the decedent or the decedent possessed the right to receive such annuity or payment, either alone or in conjunction with another, for his life or for any period not ascertainable without reference to his death or for any period which does not in fact end before his death.

(B) Division (A) of this section applies to only such part of the value of the annuity or other payment receivable under the contract or agreement as is proportionate to that part of the purchase price therefor contributed by the decedent or the decedent's employer or former employer.

(C) Notwithstanding divisions (A) and (B) of this section, the value of the gross estate does not include the value of a pension or annuity accruing to any person under federal employment, including service in the armed forces, or the value of an annuity or other payment from the police and firemen's disability and pension fund created by section 742.02 of the Revised Code, the firemen and policemen's death benefit fund created by section 742.61 of the Revised Code, the state highway patrol retirement system created by section 5505.02 of the Revised Code, the public employees retirement system created by section 145.03 of the Revised Code, the state teachers retirement system created by section 3307.03 of the Revised Code, and the school employees retirement system created by section 3309.03 of the Revised Code.

HISTORY: 132 v S 326 (Eff 7-1-68); 133 v H 1 (Eff 3-18-69); 133 v H 865 (Eff 9-4-70); 136 v S 145 (Eff 1-1-76); 136 v H 1013 (Eff 1-1-77); 140 v H 291 (Eff 7-1-83); 140 v H 794. Eff 7-6-84.

See provisions, § 127 of HB 291 (140 v —) following RC § 5731.01.

§ 5731.10 Joint and survivorship property.

(A) The value of the gross estate shall include the value of all property, to the extent of the interest therein held by the decedent and any person jointly, so that upon the death of one of them, the survivor has or the survivors have a right to the immediate ownership or possession or enjoyment of the whole property, except such part thereof as may be shown to have originally belonged to such other person or persons and never to have been received or acquired by the latter from the decedent for less than an adequate and full consideration in money or money's worth.

(B) When the person[s] holding property jointly are a husband and wife, the amount includible in the gross estate shall be one-half the value of said property. When the property has been acquired by gift, bequest, devise, or inheritance by the decedent and any other person or persons as joint owners and their interests are not otherwise specified or fixed by law, the amount includible in the gross estate shall be the value of a fractional part of said property determined by dividing the value of the property by the number of joint owners.

HISTORY: 132 v S 326. Eff 7-1-68.

§ 5731.11 Interests subject to general power of appointment.

(A) The value of the gross estate shall include the value of all property, to the extent of any interest with respect to which the decedent has on the date of the decedent's death a general power of appointment, or with respect to which the decedent has at any time exercised or released such a power of appointment by a disposition which is of such nature that if it were a transfer of property owned by the decedent, such property would be includible in the decedent's gross estate under sections 5731.05 to 5731.08, inclusive, of the Revised Code. A disclaimer or renunciation of such power of appointment shall not be deemed an exercise or a release of such power.

(B) For purposes of this section, "general power of appointment" means a power which is exercisable in favor of a decedent, his estate, his creditors, or the creditors of his estate.

(C) For the purposes of this section, if a general power of appointment created on or before October 21, 1942, has been partially or completely released so that it is no longer a general power of appointment, any such release of such power is neither the release nor the exercise of a general power of appointment if such release occurred before November 1, 1951, or the donee of such power was under a legal disability to release such power on October 21, 1942, and such release occurred not later than six months after the termination of such legal disability.

HISTORY: 132 v S 326 (Eff 7-1-68); 134 v S 398. Eff 4-1-72.

§ 5731.12 Insurance payable to estate; death benefit plans.

The value of the gross estate shall include the value of all property to the extent of the amount receivable by the decedent's estate as insurance under policies on the life of the decedent. The value of the gross estate shall not include any amount receivable as insurance under policies on the life of the decedent by beneficiaries other than the decedent's estate, whether paid directly to those beneficiaries, to a testamentary, inter vivos, or employee benefit trust for their benefit, or to a guardian or custodian for the benefit of an incompetent or minor.

HISTORY: 132 v S 326 (Eff 7-1-68); 138 v S 317 (Eff 3-23-81); 140 v H 794 (Eff 7-6-84); 141 v H 139. Eff 7-24-86.

See provisions, § 3 of HB 139 (141 v —) following RC § 5731.01.

§ 5731.13 Transfers for less than adequate consideration.

(A) If any one of the transfers, trusts, interests, rights, or powers enumerated and described in sections 5731.05 to 5731.08, inclusive and 5731.11 of the Revised Code, is made, created, exercised or relinquished for a consideration in money or money's worth, but is not a bona fide sale for an adequate and full consideration in money or money's worth, there shall be included in the gross estate only the excess of the fair market value of the property, at the time of death otherwise to be included on account of such transaction, over the value of the consideration received therefor by the decedent.

(B) For purposes of Chapter 5731. of the Revised Code, a relinquishment or promised relinquishment of dower or curtesy, or of a statutory estate created in lieu of dower or curtesy, or of other marital rights in the decedent's property or estate, shall not be considered to any extent a consideration "in money or money's worth."

HISTORY: 132 v S 326. Eff 7-1-68.

[§ 5731.13.1] § 5721.131 Income interest for life where marital deduction allowable.

Note: See following version effective 7-1-93.

(A) The value of the gross estate shall include the value of any property in which the decedent had an income interest for life if a marital deduction was allowed with respect to the transfer of such property to the decedent under section 2056(b)(7) or 2523(f) of the "Internal Revenue Code of 1986," 26 U.S.C. 2056(b)(7) and 2523(f), as amended, or if a marital deduction would have been allowed with respect to the transfer of any property in which the decedent had an income interest for life under either section if a federal estate or gift tax return were filed and any election available under either section had been made.

(B) The amendments made to this section by Substitute Senate Bill No. 336 of the 118th general assembly shall apply only to the estates of decedents who die on or after the effective date of those amendments.

HISTORY: 140 v H 291 (Eff 7-1-83); 141 v H 139 (Eff 7-24-86); 143 v H 111, § 1 (Eff 7-1-89); 143 v S 336, § 1. Eff 4-10-90.

The provisions of §§ 3–5 of S 336 (143 v —) read as follows:

SECTION 3. That the versions of sections 5731.05, 5731.131, and 5731.15 of the Revised Code that are to be effective July 1, 1993, be amended to read as follows:

[§ 5731.13.1] § 5731.131 Income interest for life where marital deduction allowable.

Note: See preceding version in effect until 7-1-93.

(A) The value of the gross estate shall include the value of any property in which the decedent had an income interest for life as follows:

(1) If a marital deduction was allowed with respect to the transfer of such property to the decedent under section 2523(f) of the "Internal Revenue Code of 1986," 26 U.S.C. 2523(f), as amended, in connection with the determination of the value of the taxable estate of the decedent's predeceasing spouse;

(2) If the decedent's predeceasing spouse was not a resident of this state at the time of his death and if a marital deduction was allowed with respect to the transfer of such property to the decedent under section 2056(b)(7) of the "Internal Revenue Code of 1986," 26 U.S.C. 2056(b)(7), as amended, in connection with the determination of the value of the taxable estate of the decedent's predeceasing spouse;

(3) If the decedent's predeceasing spouse died prior to July 1, 1993, and if a marital deduction was allowed with respect to the transfer of such property to the decedent under division (A)(1) of section 5731.15 of the Revised Code as it existed prior to July 1, 1993,

in connection with the determination of the value of the taxable estate of the decedent's predeceasing spouse;

(4) If a qualified terminable interest property deduction was allowed with respect to the transfer of such property to the decedent under division (B) of section 5731.15 of the Revised Code in connection with the determination of the value of the taxable estate of the decedent's predeceasing spouse.

(B) The amendments made to this section by Amended Substitute House Bill No. 111 and substitute Senate Bill No. 336 of the 118th general assembly that are effective on July 1, 1993, shall apply only to the estates of decedents who die on or after that date.

*HISTORY: . . . . 143 v H 111, § 3 (Eff 7-1-93); 143 v S 336, § 3. Eff 7-1-93.

SECTION 4. That all existing versions of sections 5731.05, 5731.131, and 5731.15 of the Revised Code are hereby repealed.

SECTION 5. Sections 3 and 4 of this act shall take effect on July 1, 1993.

§ 5731.14 Determination of taxable estate.

For purposes of the tax levied by section 5731.02 of the Revised Code, the value of the taxable estate shall be determined by deducting from the value of the gross estate the deductions provided for in sections 5731.15 to 5731.17 of the Revised Code.

HISTORY: 132 v S 326 (Eff 7-1-68); 132 v S 452 (Eff 7-1-68); 140 v H 291. Eff 7-1-83.

See provisions, § 127 of HB 291 (140 v —) following RC § 5731.01.

§ 5731.15 General exemptions; pay of Vietnam MIA's exempted.

Note: See following version effective 7-1-93.

For purposes of the tax levied by section 5731.02 of the Revised Code, the value of the taxable estate shall be determined by deducting from the value of the gross estate:

(A) If the decedent is survived by a spouse, a marital deduction which shall be the lesser of one of the following:

(1) If a federal estate tax return is filed and a marital deduction is taken, the amount allowed as a marital deduction by subtitle B, Chapter 11 of the Internal Revenue Code of 1986, 26 U.S.C. 2056, as amended, increased by the amount of any estate taxes imposed by this chapter by which the federal marital deduction is reduced and further increased by the value in excess of ten thousand dollars of any interest in property transferred by the decedent within a period of three years ending with the date of the decedent's death to a donee who, at the time of the decedent's death, was the spouse of the decedent, or, if a federal estate tax return is not filed and the person filing the estate tax return under this chapter does not make an election as provided in this division, the amount that would be allowed as a federal marital deduction if a federal estate tax return were filed and any election available under section 2056(b)(7) of the Internal Revenue Code of 1986, 26 U.S.C. 2056(b)(7), as amended, had been made, increased by the amount of any estate taxes imposed by this chapter by which the federal marital deduction is reduced and further increased by the value in excess of ten thousand dollars of any interest in property transferred by the decedent within a period of three years ending with the date of the decedent's death to a donee who, at the time of the decedent's death, was the spouse of the decedent.

If a federal estate tax return is not filed, the person filing the estate tax return under this chapter may elect that all or any part of the amount that would be allowed as a federal marital deduction if a federal estate tax return were filed and any election available under section 2056(b)(7) of the Internal Revenue Code of 1986, 26 U.S.C. 2056(b)(7), as amended, had been made, increased as provided in this division, is not to be taken into account in determining the marital deduction provided in division (A) of this section. The election, if desired, shall be made by the person filing the estate tax return under this chapter, in writing, on or before the date by which the return is required to be filed, determined with regard to any extension of time granted for the filing of the return. If an election as provided in this division is made, the election is irrevocable.

(2) The greater of one-half of the difference between the value of the gross estate and the deductions allowed under section 5731.16 of the Revised Code, or if the decedent dies prior to July 1, 1993, and on or after July 1, 1989, five hundred thousand dollars.

(B) The pay and allowances determined by the United States to be due to a member of the armed forces for active duty in Vietnam service for the period between the date declared by the United States as the beginning of his missing in action status to the date of his death as determined by the United States. As used in this division, "Vietnam service" means military service within the Republic of Vietnam during the period between February 28, 1961, to July 1, 1973, or military service in southeast Asia for which hostile fire pay was awarded pursuant to 37 U.S.C. 310, during the period between February 28, 1961, to July 1, 1973.

HISTORY: 132 v S 326 (Eff 7-1-68); 135 v S 1 (Eff 1-1-74); 136 v S 145 (Eff 1-1-76); 138 v H 26 (Eff 8-9-79); 139 v S 28 (Eff 10-9-81); 140 v H 291 (Eff 7-1-83); 141 v H 139 (Eff 7-24-86); 142 v H 231 (Eff 10-5-87); 142 v S 386 (Eff 3-29-88); 143 v H 111, § 1 (Eff 7-1-89); 144 v S 206. Eff 6-29-91.

The provisions of § 5 of SB 206 (144 v —) read as follows:

SECTION 5. The version of section 5731.15 of the Revised Code that results from this act is hereby repealed, effective July 1, 1993. This repeal does not affect the version of section 5731.15 of the Revised Code that is scheduled to take effect on July 1, 1993.

The provisions of §§ 3—5 of SB 336 (143 v —) read as follows:

SECTION 3. That the versions of sections 5731.05, 5731.131, and 5731.15 of the Revised Code that are to be effective July 1, 1993, be amended to read as follows:

§ 5731.15 General exemptions; pay of Vietnam MIA's exempted.

Note: See preceding version in effect until 7-1-93.

For purposes of the tax levied by section 5731.02 of the Revised Code, the value of the taxable estate shall be determined by deducting from the value of the gross estate:

(A) If the decedent dies on or after July 1, 1993 and is survived by a spouse, a marital deduction which shall be allowed in an amount equal to the value of any interest in property that passes or has passed from the decedent to the surviving spouse, but only to the extent the interest is included in the value of the gross estate. For purposes of the marital deduction, an interest in property shall be considered as passing or as having passed from the decedent to the surviving spouse only if one or more of the following apply:

(1) The interest was bequeathed or devised to the surviving spouse in the will of the decedent;

(2) The interest was inherited by the surviving spouse through intestate succession from the decedent;

(3) The interest is a dower interest of the surviving spouse, or the interest is an estate of the surviving spouse that is authorized by the Revised Code and that is in lieu of dower;

(4) The decedent transferred the interest to the surviving spouse at any time;

(5) At the time of the death of the decedent, the interest was held by the decedent and the surviving spouse, or by the decedent, the surviving spouse, and one or more other persons, in any form of joint ownership with a right of survivorship;

(6) The decedent, alone or in conjunction with any other person, had a power to appoint the interest and the interest was so appointed to the surviving spouse, or the surviving spouse acquired the interest as a result of the release or the nonexercise of the power.

(B)(1) In addition to the marital deduction provided by division (A) of this section, if an election is made in accordance with division (B)(2) of this section and the decedent dies on or after July 1, 1993, a qualified terminable interest property deduction. This deduction shall be allowed in an amount equal to all or any specific portion of qualified terminable interest property treated as separate property, but only to the extent that the property is included in the value of the gross estate.

(2) An election to have property treated as qualified terminable interest property for purposes of the deduction provided by division (B)(1) of this section shall be made by the person filing the estate tax return under this chapter, in writing, on or before the date by which the return is required to be filed, determined with regard to any extension of time granted for the filing of the return. The election shall specify whether all or only a spe-

cific portion of qualified terminable interest property treated as separate property shall be taken into account in determining the deduction. If an election as provided in this division is made, the election is irrevocable.

(3) As used in divisions (B)(1) and (2) of this section, "qualified terminable interest property" means property that satisfies all of the following:

(a) It is included in the value of the gross estate;

(b) It passes from the decedent to the surviving spouse of the decedent;

(c) It is property in which the surviving spouse of the decedent has a qualifying interest for life. For purposes of this division, the surviving spouse has a qualifying interest for life if both of the following apply:

(i) The surviving spouse is entitled to all income from the property, which income is payable annually or at more frequent intervals.

(ii) No person has a power to appoint any part of the property to any person other than the surviving spouse. This division shall not apply to a power that is exercisable only at or after the death of the surviving spouse.

(C) The pay and allowances determined by the United States to be due to a member of the armed forces for active duty in Vietnam service for the period between the date declared by the United States as the beginning of his missing in action status to the date of his death as determined by the United States. As used in this division, "Vietnam service" means military service within the Republic of Vietnam during the period between February 28, 1961, to July 1, 1973, or military service in southeast Asia for which hostile fire pay was awarded pursuant to 37 U.S.C. 310, during the period February 28, 1961, to July 1, 1973.

*HISTORY: . . . . 143 v H 111, § 3 (eff 7-1-93); 143 v S 336, § 3. Eff 7-1-93.

SECTION 4. That all existing versions of sections 5731.05, 5731.131, and 5731.15 of the Revised Code are hereby repealed.

SECTION 5. Sections 3 and 4 of this act shall take effect on July 1, 1993.

§ 5731.16 Deductions for funeral and administration expenses, and debts.

(A) For purposes of the tax levied by section 5731.02 of the Revised Code, the value of the taxable estate shall be determined by deducting from the value of the gross estate amounts for the following:

(1) Funeral expenses;

(2) Administration expenses, excluding the value of any money or property set off and allowed under section 2106.13 of the Revised Code, to the extent that such expenses have been or will be actually paid;

(3) Claims against the estate that are outstanding and unpaid as of the date of decedent's death;

(4) Unpaid mortgages on, or any indebtedness in respect of, property if the value of the decedent's interest in the property, undiminished by the mortgage or indebtedness, is included in the value of the gross estate, as are allowable by the laws of this state.

(B) There shall be deducted in determining the taxable estate amounts representing expenses incurred in administering property not subject to claims which is included in the gross estate, to the same extent such amounts would be allowable as a deduction under division (A) of this section if such property were subject to claims and such amounts are paid before the expiration of the period of limitations provided for in section 5731.38 of the Revised Code.

(C) The deduction allowed by this section in the case of claims against the estate, unpaid mortgages, or any indebtedness, when founded on a promise or agreement, is limited to the extent that they were contracted bona fide and for an adequate and full consideration in money or money's worth, except that in any case in which any such claim is founded on a promise or agreement of the decedent to make a contribution or gift to or for the use of any donee described in section 5731.17 of the Revised Code for the purposes specified in that section, the deduction is not so limited, but is limited to the extent that it would be allowable as a deduction under section 5731.17 of the Revised Code if the promise or agreement constituted a bequest.

(D) Any income taxes on income received after the death of the decedent, or property taxes not accrued before his death, or any estate, succession, legacy, or inheritance taxes, shall not be deductible under this section.

HISTORY: 132 v S 326 (Eff 7-1-68); 134 v S 398 (Eff 4-1-72); 136 v S 145 (Eff 1-1-76); 140 v H 291 (Eff 7-1-83); 143 v H 346. Eff 5-31-90.

See provisions, § 127 of HB 291 (140 v —) following RC § 5731.01.

[§ 5731.16.1] § 5731.161
Deduction from estate of transferee spouse.

(A) As used in this section:

(1) "General power of appointment" has the same meaning as in division (B) of section 5731.11 of the Revised Code.

(2) "Property" means any beneficial interest in property, whether in trust or otherwise, other than a life estate, an estate for a term of years, an annuity, or other similar interest. "Property" includes property passing as a result of the exercise or failure to exercise a power of appointment and also includes a general power of appointment.

(3) "Spousal exemption" means the exemption that was allowed to a transferor spouse's estate and that was equal to the value of any interest in property included in the value of the transferor's gross estate and transferred to or for the benefit of, and vested in, the transferee spouse, but not to exceed either sixty thousand dollars or thirty thousand dollars, whichever amount was applicable.

(4) "Transferee spouse" means the spouse who died on or after July 1, 1983, but prior to July 1, 1986, and within three years of the transferor spouse's death.

(5) "Transferor spouse" means the spouse who died prior to July 1, 1983, and within three years of the transferee spouse's death.

(B) For purposes of the tax levied by section 5731.02 of the Revised Code, the value of the taxable estate of the transferee spouse shall be determined by deducting from the value of the gross estate the value, as specified in this division, of property that was transferred to the transferee spouse by the transferor spouse and that, because of the transfer, was taxed in the estate of the transferor spouse under this chapter. The value of the property for purposes of the deduction shall be the net value of the property actually transferred, as determined and taxed in the estate of the transferor spouse, reduced by the amount of the spousal exemption with respect to the transferee spouse that was allowed in the estate of the transferor spouse, but, in any event, the value of the property for purposes of the deduction shall not exceed the greater of the following:

(1) Five hundred thousand dollars;

(2) One-half of the difference between the value of the gross estate of the transferor spouse and the deductions allowed in the estate of the transferor spouse under section 5731.16 of the Revised Code.

The deduction otherwise allowable under this section shall be reduced by the amount of the marital deduction allowed in the estate of the transferee spouse under section 5731.15 of the Revised Code.

In determining the value of the property, the value of any remainder interest, power of appointment, or similar interest shall not be reduced by the value of any intervening interest that is not considered as property for purposes of this section.

HISTORY: 140 v H 70. Eff 3-28-85.

The provisions of § 3 of HB 70 (140 v —) read as follows:

SECTION 3. The provisions of section 5731.161 of the Revised Code as enacted by this act apply to the estates of decedents who are transferee spouses and who die prior to the effective date of this act, as well as to the estates of decedents who are transferee spouses and die on or after the effective date of this act. If an estate tax return for the estate of a decedent who is a transferee spouse and who dies prior to the effective date of this act, is filed pursuant to Chapter 5731. of the Revised Code prior to that date, the executor or administrator of the decedent's estate, or other person responsible for filing the return, may file an amended return to reflect the deduction provided by section 5731.161 of the Revised Code or, if applicable, may submit a claim for refund of any estate tax paid that exceeds the estate tax payable after consideration of that deduction. An amended return or claim for refund shall be filed, within one year after the effective date of this act, in the same manner as is prescribed for the filing of an estate tax return under section 5731.21 of the Revised Code. As used in this section, "transferee spouse" has the same meaning as in section 5731.161 of the Revised Code.

§ 5731.17 Deduction for charitable bequests and transfers.

(A) For purposes of the tax levied by section 5731.02 of the Revised Code, the value of the taxable estate shall be determined by deducting from the value of the gross estate the amount of all bequests, legacies, devises, or transfers, including the interest which falls into any such bequest, legacy, devise or transfer as a result of an irrevocable disclaimer of a bequest, legacy, devise, transfer or power, if the disclaimer is made before the date prescribed for the filing of the estate tax return:

(1) To or for the use of the United States, any state, territory, any political subdivision thereof, or the District of Columbia, for exclusively public purposes;

(2) To or for the use of any corporation organized and operated exclusively for religious, charitable, scientific, literary, or educational purposes, including the encouragement of art and the prevention of cruelty to children or animals, no part of the net earnings of which inures to the benefit of any private stockholder or individual, and no substantial part of the activities of which is carrying on propaganda or otherwise attempting to influence legislation;

(3) To a trustee or trustees, or a fraternal society, order, or association operating under the lodge system, but only if such contributions or gifts are to be used by such trustee or trustees, or by such fraternal society, order, or association, exclusively for religious, charitable, scientific, literary, or educational purposes, or for the prevention of cruelty to children or animals, and no substantial part of the activities of such trustee or trustees, or of such fraternal society, order, or association, is carrying on propaganda, or otherwise attempting to influence legislation;

(4) To or for the use of any veterans' organization incorporated by act of Congress, or of its departments or local chapters or posts, no part of the net earnings of which inures to the benefit of any private shareholder or individual.

If any estate, succession, or inheritance taxes are, either by the terms of the will, by the law of the jurisdiction under which the estate is administered, or by the law of the jurisdiction imposing the particular tax, payable in whole or in part out of the bequests, legacies, or devises otherwise deductible under this section, then the amount deductible under this section shall be the amount of such bequests, legacies, or devises unreduced by the amount of such taxes.

(B) If, as of the date of a decedent's death, any bequest, legacy, devise or transfer for any of the purposes specified in division (A) of this section is dependent upon the performance of some act or the happening of a precedent event in order that it might become effective, no deduction is allowable unless the possibility that such bequest, legacy, devise or transfer will not become effective is so remote as to be negligible. The present value of a remainder, deferred payment or other limited interest shall be determined by the usual methods of valuation, including the use of tables of mortality and actuarial principles, under rules and regulations prescribed by the tax commissioner.

HISTORY: 132 v S 326. Eff 7-1-68.

§ 5731.18 Additional estate tax.

(A) In addition to the tax levied by section 5731.02 of the Revised Code, a tax is hereby levied upon the transfer of the estate of every person dying on or after July 1, 1968, who, at the time of his death was a resident of this state, in an amount equal to the maximum credit allowable by subtitle B, chapter 11 of the Internal Revenue Code of 1954, 26 U.S.C. 2011, as amended, for any taxes paid to any state.

(B) The tax levied on any estate under this section shall be credited with the amount of the tax levied under section 5731.02 of the Revised Code and with the amount of any estate, inheritance, legacy, or succession taxes actually paid to any state or territory of the United States or to the District of Columbia on any property included in the decedent's gross estate for federal estate tax purposes.

(C) The additional tax levied under this section shall be administered, collected, and paid as provided in section 5731.24 of the Revised Code.

HISTORY: 132 v S 326 (Eff 7-1-68); 140 v H 291. Eff 7-1-83.

See provisions, § 127 of HB 291 (140 v —) following RC § 5731.01.

[§ 5731.18.1] § 5731.181
Generation-skipping transfer tax.

(A) For purposes of this section, "generation-skipping transfer," "taxable distribution," and "taxable termination" have the same meaning as in Chapter 13 of subtitle B of the Internal Revenue Code of 1986, 100 Stat. 2718, 26 U.S.C. 2601-2624, as amended.

(B) A tax is hereby levied upon every generation-skipping transfer of property having a situs in this state, that occurs at the same time as, and as a result of, the death of an individual, in an amount equal to the credit allowed by Chapter 13 of subtitle B of the Internal Revenue Code of 1986, 100 Stat. 2718, 26 U.S.C. 2601-2624, as amended, for any taxes paid to any state in respect of any property included in the generation-skipping transfer.

For purposes of this division, "property having a situs in this state" includes all the following:

(1) Real property situated in this state;

(2) Tangible personal property having an actual situs in this state;

(3) Intangible personal property employed in carrying on a business in this state;

(4) Intangible personal property owned by a trust, the trustee of which resides in or has its principal place of business in this state, or, if there is more than one trustee of the trust, the principal place of administration of which is in this state.

(C) The return with respect to the generation-skipping tax levied by division (B) of this section shall be filed in the form that the tax commissioner shall prescribe, on or before the day prescribed by law, including extensions, for filing the generation-skipping transfer tax return under Chapter 13 of subtitle B of the Internal Revenue Code of 1986, 100 Stat. 2718, 26 U.S.C. 2601-2624, as amended, for the same generation-skipping transfer. The return shall be filed by the distributee in the case of a taxable distribution and by the trustee in the case of a taxable termination.

(D) The generation-skipping tax levied by division (B) of this section shall be paid, without notice or demand by the tax commissioner, with the return, and shall be charged, collected, and administered in the same manner as estate taxes levied by this chapter. This chapter is generally applicable to, except to the extent it is inconsistent with the nature of, the generation-skipping tax.

(E) If another state levies a generation-skipping tax on a transfer described in division (B) of this section, the tax commissioner may enter into a compromise of the generation-skipping tax levied by division (B) of this section in the manner provided in section 5731.35 of the Revised Code, except that no approval of any probate court is required. If such a compromise agreement is made, no interest and penalties shall accrue for the period prior to the execution of the agreement and for sixty days after its execution.

HISTORY: 140 v H 291 (Eff 7-1-83); 143 v H 286. Eff 11-8-90.

The provisions of § 3 of HB 286 (143 v —) read as follows:

SECTION 3. Sections 1 and 2 of this act apply only to the estates of decedents who die on or after the effective date of this act.

See provisions, § 127 of HB 291 (140 v —) following RC § 5731.01.

§ 5731.19 Nonresident estate tax.

(A) A tax is hereby levied upon the transfer of so much of the taxable estate of every person dying on or after July 1, 1968, who, at the time of his death, was not a resident of this state, as consists of real property situated in this state, tangible personal property having an actual situs in this state, and intangible personal property employed in carrying on a business within this state unless exempted from tax under the provisions of section 5731.34 of the Revised Code.

(B) The amount of the tax on such real and tangible personal property shall be determined as follows:

(1) Determine the amount of tax which would be payable under Chapter 5731. of the Revised Code if the decedent had died a resident of this state with all his property situated or located within this state;

(2) Multiply the tax so determined by a fraction, the denominator of which shall be the value of the gross estate wherever situated and the numerator of which shall be the said gross estate value of the real property situated and the tangible personal property having an actual situs in this state and intangible personal property employed in carrying on a business within this state and not exempted from tax under section 5731.34 of the Revised Code. The product shall be the amount of tax payable to this state.

(C) In addition to the tax levied by division (A) of this section, an additional tax is hereby levied on such real and tangible personal property determined as follows:

(1) Determine the amount of tax which would be payable under division (A) of section 5731.18 of the Revised Code, if the decedent had died a resident of this state with all his property situated or located within this state;

(2) Multiply the tax so determined by a fraction, the denominator of which shall be the value of the gross estate wherever situated and the numerator of which shall be the said gross estate value of the real property situated and the tangible property having an actual situs in this state and intangible personal property employed in carrying on a business within this state and not exempted from tax under section 5731.34 of the Revised Code. The product so derived shall be credited with the amount of the tax determined under division (B) of this section.

HISTORY: 132 v S 326. Eff 7-1-68.

§ 5731.20 Repealed, 140 v H 291, § 2 [132 v S 326; 133 v H 909; 136 v S 145]. Eff 7-1-83.

This section concerned the need for a preliminary notice and estimate of gross estate by a person or corporation required to file an estate tax return.

§ 5731.21 Estate tax return.

(A)(1)(a) Except as provided under division (A)(3) of this section, the executor or administrator, or, if no executor or administrator has been appointed, then such other person in possession of property, the transfer of which is subject to estate taxes under section 5731.02 or division (A) of section 5731.19 of the Revised Code, shall file an estate tax return, within nine months of the date of the decedent's death, in the form prescribed by the tax commissioner, in duplicate, with the probate court of the county. The return shall include all property the transfer of which is subject to estate taxes, whether such property is transferred under the last will and testament of the decedent or otherwise. The time for filing the return may be extended by the tax commissioner.

(b) The estate tax return described in division (A)(1)(a) of this section shall be accompanied by a certificate, in the form prescribed by the tax commissioner, that is signed by the executor, administrator, or other person required to file the return, and that states all of the following:

(i) The fact that the return was filed;

(ii) The date of the filing of the return;

(iii) The fact that the estate taxes under section 5731.02 or division (A) of section 5731.19 of the Revised Code, that are shown to be due in the return, have been paid in full;

(iv) If applicable, the fact that real property listed in the inventory for the decedent's estate is included in the return;

(v) If applicable, the fact that real property not listed in the inventory for the decedent's estate, including, but not limited to, survivorship tenancy property as described in section 5302.17 of the Revised Code, also is included in the return. In this regard, the certificate additionally shall describe that real property by the same description used in the return.

(2) The probate court shall forward one copy of the estate tax return described in division (A)(1)(a) of this section to the tax commissioner.

(3) If the value of the gross estate of the decedent is twenty-five thousand dollars or less and the decedent was a resident of this state, the person otherwise required to file a return may file a return, but shall not be required to do so.

(4)(a) Upon receipt of the estate tax return described in division (A)(1)(a) of this section and the accompanying certificate described in division (A)(1)(b) of

this section, the probate court promptly shall give notice of the return, by a form prescribed by the tax commissioner, to the county auditor. The auditor then shall make a charge based upon the notice and shall certify a duplicate of the charge to the county treasurer. The treasurer then shall collect, subject to division (A) of section 5731.25 of the Revised Code or any other statute extending the time for payment of an estate tax, the tax so charged.

(b) Upon receipt of the return and the accompanying certificate, the probate court also shall forward the certificate to the auditor. When satisfied that the estate taxes under section 5731.02 or division (A) of section 5731.19 of the Revised Code, that are shown to be due in the return, have been paid in full, the auditor shall stamp the certificate so forwarded to verify that payment. The auditor then shall return the stamped certificate to the probate court.

(5)(a) The certificate described in division (A)(1)(b) of this section is a public record subject to inspection and copying in accordance with section 149.43 of the Revised Code. It shall be kept in the records of the probate court pertaining to the decedent's estate and is not subject to the confidentiality provisions of section 5731.90 of the Revised Code.

(b) All persons are entitled to rely on the statements contained in a certificate as described in division (A)(1)(b) of this section if it has been filed in accordance with that division, forwarded to a county auditor and stamped in accordance with division (A)(4) of this section, and placed in the records of the probate court pertaining to the decedent's estate in accordance with division (A)(5)(a) of this section. The real property referred to in the certificate shall be free of, and may be regarded by all persons as being free of, any lien for estate taxes under section 5731.02 and division (A) of section 5731.19 of the Revised Code.

(B) An estate tax return filed under this section, in the form prescribed by the tax commissioner, and showing that no estate tax is due shall result in a determination that no estate tax is due, if the tax commissioner within three months after the receipt of the return by the department of taxation, fails to file exceptions to the return in the probate court of the county in which the return was filed. A copy of exceptions to such a return, when the tax commissioner files them within that period, shall be sent by ordinary mail to the person who filed the return. The tax commissioner is not bound under this division by a determination that no estate tax is due, with respect to property not disclosed in the return.

(C) If the executor, administrator, or other person required to file an estate tax return fails to file it within nine months of the date of the decedent's death, the tax commissioner may determine the estate tax in such estate and issue a certificate of determination in the same manner as is provided in division (B) of section 5731.27 of the Revised Code. Such certificate of determination has the same force and effect as though a return had been filed and a certificate of determination issued with respect to the return.

HISTORY: 132 v S 326 (Eff 7-1-68); 134 v S 413 (Eff 4-1-72); 137 v H 826 (Eff 1-1-79); 139 v S 28 (Eff 10-9-81); 140 v H 291 (Eff 7-1-83); 141 v H 139 (Eff 7-24-86); 143 v H 286. Eff 11-8-90.

See provisions, § 3 of HB 286 (143 v —) following RC § 5731.18.1.

See provisions, § 3 of HB 139 (141 v —) following RC § 5731.01.

See provisions, § 4 of HB 139 (141 v —) following RC § 5731.15.

See provisions, § 5 of HB 139 (141 v —) following RC § 5731.13.1.

§ 5731.22 Failure to file preliminary notice; penalties.

If the executor, administrator, or other person required to file a return fails to file the return required by this chapter on the date prescribed therefor,

determined with regard to any extension of time for filing, unless it is shown that such failure is due to reasonable cause and not due to willful neglect, there shall be added to the amount of tax as finally determined a penalty determined by the tax commissioner, in the amount of five per cent of the amount of that tax if the failure is not for more than one month, or, if the failure is for more than one month, in the amount of five per cent of the amount of that tax plus an additional five per cent for each additional month or fraction of a month during which the failure continues, not exceeding twenty-five per cent in the aggregate. If, due to fraud, there is a failure to file the return or an underpayment of tax due under this chapter, there shall be added to the amount of tax as finally determined a penalty determined by the tax commissioner, in an amount not to exceed ten thousand dollars. The penalties imposed by this section shall be collected at the same time and in the same manner as the tax itself.

The penalties shall be charged against the executor, administrator, or other person having custody or control of any property the transfer of which is subject to estate tax, and such executor, administrator, or other person is personally liable for the penalties. Such penalties shall be divided in the same manner prescribed for the division of the tax in sections 5731.50 and 5731.51 of the Revised Code.

HISTORY: 132 v S 326 (Eff 7-1-68); 140 v H 291. Eff 7-1-83.

See provisions, § 127 of HB 291 (140 v —) following RC § 5731.01.

§ 5731.23 Due date of tax; interest on late payment or overpayment.

Subject to division (A) of section 5731.25 of the Revised Code or any other statute extending the time for payment of an estate tax, the tax levied by section 5731.02 and division (A) of section 5731.19 of the Revised Code shall, without notice or demand by the tax commissioner, be due and payable by the person liable for it, at the expiration of nine months from the date of the decedent's death, to the treasurer of the county. If any amount of tax levied by section 5731.02 or division (A) of section 5731.19 of the Revised Code is not paid on or before nine months from the date of the decedent's death, interest on such amount shall be paid for the period from such date to the date paid, computed at the rate per annum prescribed by section 5703.47 of the Revised Code. Interest at the same rate shall be paid on any amount of tax determined to be due by way of deficiency from nine months from the date of the decedent's death to the date of payment thereof. Such interest shall be charged and collected in the same manner as the tax.

Interest computed at the rate per annum prescribed by section 5703.47 of the Revised Code shall be allowed and paid upon any overpayment of tax levied by section 5731.02 or division (A) of section 5731.19 of the Revised Code from nine months from the date of the decedent's death or the date of payment of the tax, whichever is later, to the date such overpayment is repaid. Such payment may be made upon an estimated basis whether or not a return is filed, and shall be charged and collected in the same manner as provided in section 5731.21 of the Revised Code.

At any time after nine months from the date of the decedent's death, payment of an estimated deficiency may be made and shall be credited against any deficiency of tax finally determined. Interest on any deficiency ultimately determined to be due shall be charged only upon the unpaid portion thereof.

HISTORY: 132 v S 326 (Eff 7-1-68); 132 v S 452 (Eff 7-1-68); 134 v S 413 (Eff 4-1-72); 139 v S 530 (Eff 6-25-82); 141 v H 139. Eff 7-24-86.

See provisions, § 3 of HB 139 (141 v —) following RC § 5731.01.

[§ 5731.23.1] § 5731.231
Repealed, 141 v H 139, § 2 [140 v H 291; 140 v H 794]. Eff 7-24-86.

This section concerned interest in closely held business and installment payments.

§ 5731.24 Time for return and payment of additional tax.

If an additional tax prescribed by section 5731.18 of the Revised Code is due, the executor, administrator, or other person required to file the estate tax return, within sixty days after the date of the final determination of the federal estate tax liability, shall file an additional tax return, in the form prescribed by the tax commissioner, in the same manner as is prescribed for the filing of the estate tax return. Subject to division (A) of section 5731.25 of the Revised Code or any other statute extending the time for payment of an estate tax, the additional tax shall be paid, without notice or demand by the tax commissioner, with the return, and shall be charged and collected in the same manner as the estate tax, except that no interest shall accrue until sixty days after the date of the final determination of the federal estate tax liability.

HISTORY: 132 v S 326 (Eff 7-1-68); 141 v H 139. Eff 7-24-86.

See provisions, § 3 of HB 139 (141 v —) following RC § 5731.01.

§ 5731.25 Extension of time for payment of estate tax when undue hardship is involved; postponement of payment; interest; bond.

(A)(1) As used in this division, "undue hardship" means that any of the following applies:

(a) There is difficulty in marshalling liquid assets of the gross estate that are located in several jurisdictions;

(b) A substantial portion of the assets

of the gross estate consists of rights to receive payments in the future, including, but not limited to, annuities, copyright royalties, contingent fees, and accounts receivable;

(c) The size of the gross estate cannot be determined accurately because a claim to substantial assets of the decedent is subject to litigation;

(d) Despite reasonable efforts to convert assets of the gross estate into cash, there are not sufficient liquid funds in the gross estate to pay the entire amount of an estate tax imposed by this chapter when it is due, to provide for the reasonable needs of the widow and dependent children of the decedent during the remaining period of the administration of the estate, and to pay claims against the estate that are due and payable;

(e) A significant portion of the gross estate consists of a farm or a closely-held business, and there are not readily available, sufficient funds in the gross estate to pay an estate tax imposed by this chapter and any federal estate tax. For purposes of this division, funds shall not be considered readily available because the farm or closely-held business could be sold to persons who are not related by consanguinity or affinity to the decedent, at a price that equals the fair market value of the farm or closely-held business.

(f) Assets in the gross estate that would have to be liquidated to pay an estate tax imposed by this chapter when due, only could be sold at a price that is considered a sacrifice price or only could be sold in a depressed market.

(g) Other circumstances exist as specified by a rule of the tax commissioner. The tax commissioner may adopt rules that specify circumstances not described in divisions (A)(1)(a) to (f) of this section that he considers constitute undue hardship.

(2) If an estate tax return is filed pursuant to this chapter and estate tax due, including a deficiency in tax, cannot be paid in whole or in part because of undue hardship to the estate or a person required to pay tax, the tax commissioner shall extend the time for payment of the tax or a portion of it for a period or periods, subject to the limitations set forth in this division. The maximum time of one period of extension shall be one year, and the maximum time of all periods of extension shall be fourteen years. The tax commissioner shall prescribe rules that govern extensions authorized by this division.

(B) If the value of a reversionary or remainder interest in property is included under this chapter in the value of the gross estate, the payment of the part of the tax imposed by this chapter attributable to such interest may, at the election of the executor, administrator, or any other person liable for such tax, be postponed until six months after the termination of the precedent interest or interests in property. The amount, the payment of which is so postponed, shall bear interest at the rate of three per cent per annum from the date fixed for payment of the tax, which interest shall be paid by the person liable for the tax in addition to the tax. The postponement of such amount shall be under rules prescribed by the tax commissioner, and shall be upon condition that the executor, administrator, or any other person liable for the tax, gives bond to the county treasurer in such amount, and with such sureties as the tax commissioner considers necessary, conditioned upon the payment within six months after the termination of such precedent interest or interests of the amount, the payment of which is so postponed, together with interest on it, as provided in this division.

HISTORY: 132 v S 326 (Eff 7-1-68); 141 v H 139. Eff 7-24-86.

See provisions, § 3 of HB 139 (141 v —) following RC § 5731.01.

§ 5731.26 Duties and powers of tax commissioner.

(A) The tax commissioner shall promptly determine the correctness of the return with respect to the includibility of property, the fair market value or, if applicable, the actual qualified use value of the assets included in the gross estate, the allowance of the credit against the tax and deductions, and all other matters necessary to determine the correct amount of the tax. For this purpose, he may issue subpoenas, compel the attendance of witnesses and the production of books and papers, examine the witnesses under oath concerning any relevant matter, and require the submission of affidavits and forms which he may deem necessary to determine the correct amount of the tax.

The tax commissioner may designate an employee or employees of the county auditor or of the probate court of any county, with the consent of the county auditor or of the probate judge of that county, as his agent or agents to assist him in accepting filings of returns in the county, in determining the correctness of the returns filed in the county, and in complying with this chapter. The employee or employees so designated shall have all of the powers granted to the tax commissioner for these purposes.

(B) The tax commissioner shall give notice to the person filing the return of any adjustments which he proposes to make, and, at the request of the person, shall set a time for an administrative conference on the notice in the county or, by agreement of the person filing the return and the tax commissioner, in Columbus. At the conclusion of such conference, or if the conference is waived by the person filing the return, the tax commissioner shall proceed with the final determination of the tax liability as provided in section 5731.27 of the Revised Code.

(C) At or before the time of the administrative conference, the person filing the return and the tax commissioner may agree in writing to have the correctness of the return as to any item determined in accordance with the final determination of such item for federal estate tax purposes. If such agreement is made, the person filing the return shall, within sixty days after the final determination of the federal estate tax liability, furnish to the tax commissioner such information as may be required to determine the tax in accordance with such agreement, and the tax commissioner shall make his final determination of tax liability in the same manner as is provided in section 5731.27 of the Revised Code.

HISTORY: 132 v S 326 (Eff 7-1-68); 140 v H 291. Eff 7-1-83.

See provisions, § 127 of HB 291 (140 v —) following RC § 5731.01.

§ 5731.27 Certificate of determination of tax liability; deficiency; refund.

(A) The tax commissioner shall, if he determines that a return indicating that a tax is due is correct as filed, issue a certificate of determination of final estate tax liability showing the amount of such liability, if any, in triplicate, one copy of which shall be sent by regular mail to the person filing the return, one copy of which shall be sent to the county auditor for the county in which the return was filed, and one copy of which shall be sent to the probate court of the county in which the return was filed if there is an administration of or other proceedings in the decedent's estate.

(B) The tax commissioner, if he determines a deficiency or refund of tax or penalty addition to tax, shall issue his certificate of determination stating the adjusted amount of the tax due and the amount of any refund, deficiency, or penalty. Such certificate also shall state whether or not any portion of the tax liability has been reserved for later determination in accordance with division (C) of section 5731.26 of the Revised Code. Such certificate shall be issued in triplicate, one copy of which shall be sent by certified mail, return receipt requested, to the person filing the return, or to the person required to file the return if no such return was filed, one copy of which shall be sent to the county auditor for the county in which the return was filed or was required to be filed, and one copy of which shall be sent to the probate court for the county in which the return was filed or required to be filed if there will be an administration of or other proceedings in the decedent's estate. The person required to file the return, or any interested party, shall have sixty days from the date of receipt of such certificate by the person required to file the return within which to file exceptions to such determination as provided in section 5731.30 of the Revised Code.

(C) The county auditor, if no exceptions have been filed within the time specified in division (B) of this section, or if the right to file exceptions has been waived by all interested parties by written waivers filed with the county auditor, shall:

(1) If the certificate of determination is for a refund, draw his warrant for the proper amount of the refund and interest on it, which warrant shall be paid by the county treasurer out of any money in his possession to the credit of estate taxes;

(2) If the certificate of determination is for a deficiency or penalty, make a charge based upon such determination, and certify a duplicate of it to the county treasurer, who shall collect, subject to division (A) of section 5731.25 of the Revised Code or any other statute extending the time for payment of an estate tax, the deficiency or penalty so charged.

HISTORY: 132 v S 326 (Eff 7-1-68); 141 v H 139. Eff 7-24-86.

See provisions, § 3 of HB 139 (141 v —) following RC § 5731.01.

§ 5731.28 Refund; time for filing claim.

If any debts deductible under section 5731.16 of the Revised Code are proved

against the gross estate after the tax levied by section 5731.02 or division (A) of section 5731.19 of the Revised Code has been determined, or if the determination of taxes so made is erroneous due to a mistake of fact or law, a claim for refund of tax may be filed by an executor, administrator, trustee, person in possession of property subject to tax, or any transferee thereof, within three years from the time the return was required to be filed (determined without regard to any extension of time for filing), in the form prescribed by the tax commissioner. The claim for refund shall be filed in the same manner as is prescribed for the filing of a return in section 5731.21 of the Revised Code and the determination of its correctness shall be made in the same manner as is provided for in the case of the return itself.

HISTORY: 132 v S 326 (Eff 7-1-68); 136 v S 466. Eff 5-26-76.

§ 5731.29 Repealed, 133 v S 319, § 1 [132 v S 326]. Eff 11-18-69.

This section referred to filing final determination of estate taxes.

§ 5731.30 Appeal to probate court from determination of tax commissioner; notice; hearing.

The tax commissioner, the person required to file the return, or any interested party may file exceptions in writing to the tax commissioner's final determination of taxes, with the probate court of the county. Exceptions shall be filed within sixty days from the receipt of the certificate of determination issued by the tax commissioner, stating the grounds upon which such exceptions are taken. The court shall, by order, fix a time, not less than ten days thereafter, for the hearing of such exceptions, and shall give such notice of that hearing as it considers necessary, provided, that a copy of such notice and of such exceptions shall be forthwith mailed to the tax commissioner. Upon the hearing of such exceptions, the court may make a just and proper order. No costs shall be allowed by the court on such exceptions.

In a like manner, exceptions may be filed to the disallowance or partial disallowance of any claim for refund of taxes filed pursuant to section 5731.28 of the Revised Code.

Upon redetermination of taxes pursuant to this section, if no appeal is taken from the redetermination, the tax commissioner shall issue his certificate of determination of taxes reflecting the corrected determination in the same manner as is provided in section 5731.27 of the Revised Code.

HISTORY: 132 v S 326 (Eff 7-1-68); 141 v H 139. Eff 7-24-86.

See provisions, § 3 of HB 139 (141 v —) following RC § 5731.01.

[§ 5731.30.1] § 5731.301

Repealed, 134 v H 1, § 2 [132 v S 327]. Eff 3-26-71.

This section referred to compromise settlement.

§ 5731.31 Duties of probate court.

The probate court of the county has jurisdiction to determine all questions concerning the administration of the taxes levied by this chapter, and all questions concerning the proper determination of the amount of such taxes or penalties upon exceptions filed as provided in section 5731.30 of the Revised Code. Such jurisdiction shall exist not only as to the transfer of property which would otherwise invoke the jurisdiction of such court, but shall extend to all cases covered by this chapter, so that all transfers, taxable under this chapter, whether made under the last will and testament of the decedent or otherwise, shall be within such jurisdiction.

HISTORY: 132 v S 326 (Eff 7-1-68); 141 v H 139. Eff 7-24-86.

See provisions, § 3 of HB 139 (141 v —) following RC § 5731.01.

§ 5731.32 Appeal from final order of probate court.

An appeal may be taken by any party, including the tax commissioner, from the final order of the probate court under section 5731.30 of the Revised Code in the manner provided by law for appeals from orders of the probate court in other cases. An appeal by the tax commissioner may be perfected in the manner provided by law.

Upon redetermination of taxes pursuant to this section, the tax commissioner shall issue his certificate of determination of taxes reflecting the corrected determination thereof in the same manner as is provided in section 5731.27 of the Revised Code.

HISTORY: 132 v S 326. Eff 7-1-68.

§ 5731.33 Payment; receipts; duties of county treasurer; prohibitions.

(A)(1) Upon the payment to the county treasurer of any tax due under this chapter, the treasurer shall issue a receipt for the payment in triplicate. He shall deliver one copy to the person paying the taxes, and he immediately shall send the original receipt to the tax commissioner, who shall certify the original receipt and immediately transmit it to the probate court for the county in which the return has been filed if there is an administration of or other proceedings in the decedent's estate.

(2) Upon the payment to a county treasurer of all estate taxes due under section 5731.02 or division (A) of section 5731.19 of the Revised Code with respect to a particular decedent's estate, the treasurer, in order to assist the county auditor in performing his responsibility under division (A)(4)(b) of section 5731.21 of the Revised Code, also shall notify the auditor, in writing, of the full payment of those taxes.

(B) An executor, administrator, or testamentary trustee is not entitled to credits in his accounts and is not entitled to be discharged from liability for taxes due under this chapter, and the estate under his control shall not be distributed, unless a certified receipt has been filed with the probate court as described in division (A)(1) of this section.

(C) Any person, upon the payment of one dollar to a county treasurer issuing a receipt as described in division (A)(1) of this section, shall be entitled to a duplicate receipt, executed in the same manner as the original receipt.

HISTORY: 132 v S 326 (Eff 7-1-68); 141 v H 139 (Eff 7-24-86); 143 v H 268. Eff 11-8-90.

See provisions, § 3 of HB 268 (143 v —) following RC § 5731.18.1.

See provisions, § 3 of HB 139 (141 v —) following RC § 5731.01.

§ 5731.34 Tax imposed on transfers of intangible personal property employed in business; reciprocity.

No estate or additional tax shall be imposed upon any transfer of intangible personal property by or from a person who was not legally domiciled in this state at the time of his death, or by reason of the death of such a person, whether such person was the legal or the beneficial owner of such property, and whether or not such property was held for him in this state or elsewhere by another, in trust or otherwise, unless such property was employed by such nonresident in carrying on business within this state. No estate or additional tax shall be imposed upon the transfer of intangible personal property in any case if the laws of the state, territory, or country of domicile of the transferor at the time of his death contained a reciprocal exemption provision under which nonresidents were exempted from transfer or death taxes of every character on personal property, except tangible personal property having an actual situs therein, if the state, territory, or country of domicile of such nonresident allowed a similar exemption to residents of the state, territory, or country of domicile of such transferor.

HISTORY: 132 v S 326 (Eff 7-1-68); 133 v H 1. Eff 3-18-69.

§ 5731.35 Foreign estate taxes; compromise.

When a probate court or the tax commissioner determines or claims that a decedent was domiciled in this state at the date of decedent's death, and when the taxing authorities of another state, territory, or possession of the United States, or the District of Columbia, make a like claim on behalf of their state, territory, or possession of the United States, or the District of Columbia, the tax commissioner, with the approval of the probate court having jurisdiction of the estate, may enter into a written agreement or compromise with the taxing authorities of such other state, territory, or possession of the United States, or the District of Columbia, and the executor, administrator, or personal representatives of the estate, that a certain amount may be accepted in full satisfaction of any and all estate and additional taxes imposed under Chapter 5731. of the Revised Code, including any interest or penalties accruing to the date of the signing of the agreement. The agreement shall also fix the amount to be accepted by the taxing authorities of such other state, territory, or possession of the United States, or the District of Columbia, in full satisfaction of their inheritance, succession, and estate taxes. Unless the amount of the tax, so agreed upon, is paid within sixty days after the date of execution of the agreement, interest and penalties, as provided under Chapter 5731. of the Revised Code, shall thereafter accrue upon the amount fixed in the agreement, but the time between fifteen months from the date of decedent's death and the signing of such agreement, shall not be included in computing interest or penalties.

HISTORY: 132 v S 326. Eff 7-1-68.

§ 5731.36 Administrator of foreign death tax laws deemed creditor of decedent; reciprocity.

(A) The official or body charged with the administration of the estate or other death tax laws of the domiciliary state of a nonresident decedent is deemed a creditor of the decedent and may sue in the courts of this state and enforce any claim for taxes, penalties, and interest due to that state or a political subdivision of that state. This section applies to the estate of a decedent not domiciled in this state only if the laws of his domicile state contain a provision, of any nature, by which this state is given reasonable assurance of the collection of its estate and other death taxes, interest, and penalties from the estates of decedents dying domiciled in this state.

(B) This section does not apply to the generation-skipping tax levied by division (B) of section 5731.181 of the Revised Code.

(C) This section shall be liberally construed in order to ensure that the state of domicile of a decedent receives any estate or other death taxes, interest, and penalties due it from the decedent's estate.

(D) As used in this section, "state" includes any state or territory of the United States, the District of Columbia, and Canada or any province of Canada.

HISTORY: 132 v S 326 (Eff 7-1-68); 143 v H 286. Eff 11-8-90.

See provisions, § 3 of HB 286 (143 v —) following RC § 5731.18.1.

§ 5731.37 Taxes are lien; liability of executor, administrator, trustee or person in possession of property.

(A) Taxes levied by this chapter shall be, until restricted, transferred, or discharged pursuant to this division, until paid, or unless division (A)(5)(b) of section 5731.21 of the Revised Code applies to them, a lien upon all property subject to the taxes. This lien:

(1) Is discharged, as to property applied to costs and expenses of administration, property constituting the allowance made to the surviving spouse, minor children, or surviving spouse and minor children of the decedent under section 2106.13 of the Revised Code for their support, and all of the property of a decedent that is subject to inclusion in the gross estate and that has been disclosed to the tax commissioner by the time a certificate of discharge is issued;

(2) Is transferred, to the extent of any such property sold by the executor, administrator, or trustee for the purpose of paying debts, administration expenses, or taxes of the estate, or for any purpose to a bona fide purchaser for an adequate and full consideration in money or money's worth, to the money or other property received from the purchaser. Knowledge that the property is being sold by a fiduciary and that it otherwise would be subject to the estate tax lien does not preclude the purchaser from being classified as a bona fide purchaser.

(3) May be, by written authorization of the tax commissioner, restricted to all property that is subject to such taxes, and not specifically released, transferred to other property on conditions acceptable to the tax commissioner, or fully discharged, each upon conditions, including payment of a reasonable fee, prescribed by rules adopted under section 5703.14 of the Revised Code, when he determines that any of these actions will not jeopardize the collection of the taxes;

(4) Shall be restricted, transferred, or discharged, as authorized in division (A)(3) of this section, by the tax commissioner, upon order of the probate court after notice to the commissioner and any other person whose substantial rights may reasonably be affected by the lien and hearing on an application of the executor, administrator, trustee, or the owner of an interest in any property subject, or reasonably the object of a claim to be subject, to the lien, and proof that

the collection of the taxes will not be jeopardized by the action, and that the tax commissioner failed to grant a reasonable request for the action within sixty days of his receipt of a written request.

(B) The executor, administrator, trustee, or other person in possession of property, the transfer of which is subject to the taxes, or any transferee of the property, except a bona fide purchaser for an adequate and full consideration in money or money's worth, is personally liable for all the taxes to the extent that their collection is reduced by his omission to perform a statutory duty, with interest as provided in section 5731.23 of the Revised Code, until they have been paid. An administrator, executor, or trustee of any property, the transfer of which is subject to the taxes shall deduct the taxes from the property, or collect them from any person entitled to the property. He shall not deliver or be compelled to deliver any property, the transfer of which is subject to the taxes, to any person, until the taxes on it have been collected, and on any other property of the same decedent that has been, or is to be, transferred to the person or his spouse or minor child. He may sell so much of the estate of the decedent as will enable him to pay the taxes in the same manner as for the payment of the debts of the decedent. Knowledge that the property is being sold by a fiduciary and that it otherwise would be subject to the estate tax lien does not preclude the purchaser from being classified as a bona fide purchaser.

(C) If an election is made, pursuant to division (B)(1)(b) or (c) of section 5731.011 of the Revised Code to have qualified farm property valued at its value for actual qualified use, an amount equivalent to the estate tax savings realized in the decedent's estate by valuating the property at its value for its actual qualified use, instead of at its fair market value pursuant to division (B) of section 5731.01 of the Revised Code, shall be a lien in favor of this state on the property for four years after the decedent's death, unless it is earlier discharged. The tax commissioner may issue a certificate of subordination of any lien imposed by this division upon any part of the property subject to the lien, if the tax commissioner determines that the state will be adequately secured after the subordination.

HISTORY: 132 v S 326 (Eff 7-1-68); 134 v S 398 (Eff 4-1-72); 136 v S 145 (Eff 1-1-76); 139 v S 28 (Eff 10-9-81); 141 v H 139 (Eff 7-24-86); 143 v H 346 (Eff 5-31-90); 143 v H 286. Eff 11-8-90.

See provisions, § 3 of HB 286 (143 v —) following RC § 5731.18.1.

See provisions, § 3 of HB 139 (141 v —) following RC § 5731.01.

§ 5731.38 Limitation on time for determining tax liability.

No liability for the payment of taxes levied under Chapter 5731. of the Revised Code, including all interest and penalties thereon, may be determined as to the return required to be filed under section 5731.21 of the Revised Code, subsequent to three years after such return is filed, and as to the return required to be filed under section 5731.24 of the Revised Code, subsequent to three years after such return is filed. Any lien in realty created under Chapter 5731. of the Revised Code shall become void upon the expiration of ten years after the date of decedent's death.

In the event there is litigation pending at the expiration of such three-year period for the determination or collection of any such tax, including interest or penalties thereon, the liability for the payment thereof continues until the expiration of one year after final determination of such litigation.

HISTORY: 132 v S 326 (Eff 7-1-68); 134 v S 186. Eff 3-20-72.

§ 5731.39 Release of assets; consent to transfer; exceptions.

(A) No corporation organized or existing under the laws of this state shall transfer on its books or issue a new certificate for any share of its capital stock registered in the name of a decedent, or in trust for a decedent, or in the name of a decedent and another person or persons, without the written consent of the tax commissioner.

(B) No safe deposit company, trust company, financial institution as defined in division (A) of section 5725.01 of the Revised Code or other corporation or person, having in possession, control, or custody a deposit standing in the name of a decedent, or in trust for a decedent, or in the name of a decedent and another person or persons, shall deliver or transfer an amount in excess of three-fourths of the total value of such deposit, including accrued interest and dividends, as of the date of decedent's death, without the written consent of the tax commissioner. The written consent of the tax commissioner need not be obtained prior to the delivery or transfer of amounts having a value of three-fourths or less of said total value.

(C) No life insurance company shall pay the proceeds of an annuity or matured endowment contract, or of a life insurance contract payable to the estate of a decedent, or of any other insurance contract taxable under Chapter 5731. of the Revised Code, without the written consent of the tax commissioner. Any life insurance company may pay the proceeds of any insurance contract not specified in this division (C) without the written consent of the tax commissioner.

(D) No trust company or other corporation or person shall pay the proceeds of any death benefit, retirement, pension or profit sharing plan in excess of two thousand dollars, without the written consent of the tax commissioner. Such trust company or other corporation or person, however, may pay the proceeds of any death benefit, retirement, pension, or profit-sharing plan which consists of insurance on the life of the decedent payable to a beneficiary other than the estate of the insured without the written consent of the tax commissioner.

(E) No safe deposit company, trust company, financial institution as defined in division (A) of section 5725.01 of the Revised Code, or other corporation or person, having in possession, control, or custody securities, assets, or other property (including the shares of the capital stock of, or other interest in, such safe deposit company, trust company, financial institution as defined in division (A) of section 5725.01 of the Revised Code, or other corporation), standing in the name of a decedent, or in trust for a decedent, or in the name of a decedent and another person or persons, and the transfer of which is taxable under Chapter 5731. of the Revised Code, shall deliver or transfer any such securities, assets, or other property which have a value as of the date of decedent's death in excess of three-fourths of the total value thereof, without the written consent of the tax commissioner. The written consent of the tax commissioner need not be obtained prior to the delivery or transfer of any such securities, assets, or other property having a value of three-fourths or less of said total value.

(F) No safe deposit company, financial institution as defined in division (A) of section 5725.01 of the Revised Code, or other corporation or person having possession or control of a safe deposit box or similar receptacle standing in the name of a decedent or in the name of the decedent and another person or persons, or to which the decedent had a right of access, except when such safe deposit box or other receptacle stands in the name of a corporation or partnership, or in the name of the decedent as guardian or executor, shall deliver any of the contents thereof unless the safe deposit box or similar receptacle has been opened and inventoried in the presence of the tax commissioner or his agent, and a written consent to transfer issued; provided, however, that a safe deposit company, financial institution, or other corporation or person having possession or control of a safe deposit box may deliver wills, deeds to burial lots, and insurance policies to a representative of the decedent, but that a representative of the safe deposit company, financial institution, or other corporation or person must supervise the opening of the box and make a written record of the wills, deeds, and policies removed. Such written record shall be included in the tax commissioner's inventory records.

(G) Notwithstanding any provision of this section, the tax commissioner may authorize any delivery or transfer or waive any of the foregoing requirements under such terms and conditions as he may prescribe. Failure to comply with this section shall render such safe deposit company, trust company, life insurance company, financial institution as defined in division (A) of section 5725.01 of the Revised Code, or other corporation or person liable for the amount of the taxes and interest due under the provisions of Chapter 5731. of the Revised Code on the transfer of such stock, deposit, proceeds of an annuity or matured endowment contract or of a life insurance contract payable to the estate of a decedent, or other insurance contract taxable under Chapter 5731. of the Revised Code, proceeds of any death benefit, retirement, pension, or profit sharing plan in excess of two thousand dollars, or securities, assets, or other property of any resident decedent, and in addition thereto, to a penalty of not less than five hundred or more than five thousand dollars.

HISTORY: 132 v S 326 (Eff 7-1-68); 139 v H 816. Eff 3-4-83.

§ 5731.40 Transfer of assets of nonresident decedent.

The consent of the tax commissioner is not required in the case of the issuance or transfer or delivery of any intangible personal property specified in section 5731.39 of the Revised Code, when the decedent is not domiciled in this state.

In any action brought under section 5731.39 of the Revised Code, it shall be sufficient defense that the issuance or transfer or delivery of any such property was made in good faith and without knowledge or circumstances sufficient to place the defendant on inquiry as to the domicile of the decedent.

HISTORY: 132 v S 326. Eff 7-1-68.

§ 5731.41 Appointment of agents by tax commissioner; compensation.

To enforce section 5731.39 of the Revised Code, the tax commissioner may appoint agents in the unclassified civil service who shall perform such duties as are prescribed by the commissioner. Such agents shall, as compensation, receive annually eight cents per capita for each full one thousand of the first twenty thousand of the population of the county and two cents per capita for each full one thousand over twenty thousand of the population of the county, as shown by the last federal census, which shall be paid in equal monthly installments from the undivided inheritance or estate tax in the county treasury on the warrant of the county auditor, any other provision of law to the contrary notwithstanding. The amount paid to any agent in the unclassified service for duties performed in estate tax matters, as directed by the commissioner, shall not exceed three thousand nor be less than twelve hundred dollars in any calendar year.

HISTORY: 132 v S 326. Eff 12-1-67.

The provisions of § 9 of HB 897 (140 v —) read as follows:

SECTION 9. In addition to the compensation as set forth in section 5731.41 of the Revised Code and notwithstanding any limitations set forth in that section, those agents appointed by the tax commissioner pursuant to that section for calendar year 1985 located in a county with a population of one to seventy thousand shall receive as compensation three thousand dollars; those agents located in a county with a population of seventy thousand one to one hundred five thousand shall receive as compensation five thousand dollars; and those agents located in a county with a population of one hundred five thousand one and over shall receive as compensation seven thousand dollars. In calendar year 1986, each such agent appointed by the tax commissioner for that year shall receive as compensation an amount equal to twice the total compensation computed under this section for an agent located in that county for calendar year 1985. All such payments shall be made in the same manner as provided in section 5731.41 of the Revised Code.

See **Comment,** Legislative Service Commission, following RC § 5705.22.1.

§ 5731.42 Collection of tax; proceedings; duties of attorney general.

If, after the determination of any tax levied under this chapter, such tax remains unpaid, the tax commissioner shall notify the attorney general in writing of the nonpayment. The attorney general shall obtain from the tax commissioner a certified copy of the certificate of determination of the tax. Such certified copy of the certificate of determination of the tax shall be filed in the office of the clerk of the court of common pleas of the county, and the same proceedings shall be had with respect thereto as are provided by section 2329.04 of the Revised Code with respect to transcripts of judgments rendered by judges of the county courts, except that the attorney general shall not be required to pay the costs accruing at the time of filing the certified copy. The same effect shall be given to such certified copy of the certificate of determination of the tax for all purposes as is given to such transcripts of judgments of judges of the county courts filed in like manner. This section does not affect the date of the lien of such taxes on the property passing, or divest such lien before the payment of such tax in the event of failure to seek out execution within the period prescribed by section 2329.07 of the Revised Code.

HISTORY: 132 v S 326 (Eff 7-1-68); 140 v H 291. Eff 7-1-83.

See provisions, § 127 of HB 291 (140 v —) following RC § 5731.01.

§ 5731.43 Attorney general to represent state; appointment of attorney employed by department of taxation.

The attorney general, when requested by the tax commissioner, shall represent the state, the tax commissioner, and the county auditor in any proceedings under Chapter 5731. of the Revised Code. The tax commissioner, with the consent of the attorney general, may designate any attorney assigned to or employed by the estate tax division of the Department of Taxation to represent the tax commissioner, and no additional compensation shall be paid to any attorney so designated for services performed in such capacity.

HISTORY: 132 v S 326. Eff 7-1-68.

§ 5731.44 County auditor; appointment of deputies.

The county auditor may, and when directed by the tax commissioner shall, appoint such number of deputies as the tax commissioner prescribes for him, who shall be qualified to assist him in the performance of his duties under Chapter 5731. of the Revised Code.

HISTORY: 132 v S 326. Eff 7-1-68.

§ 5731.45 Administration of tax; appointment of assistants.

The tax commissioner may designate such of his examiners, experts, accountants, and other assistants as he deems necessary for the purpose of aiding in the administration of taxes levied under Chapter 5731. of the Revised Code; and the provisions of Chapter 5731. of the Revised Code shall be deemed a law which the tax commissioner is required to administer for the purposes of sections 5703.17 to 5703.37, inclusive, 5703.39, and 5703.41 of the Revised Code. The tax commissioner shall in the administration of the taxes levied under Chapter 5731. of the Revised Code see that the proceedings are instituted and carried to determination in all cases in which a tax is due.

The tax commissioner may adopt and promulgate regulations not inconsistent with sections 5731.01 to 5731.52, inclusive, of the Revised Code.

HISTORY: 132 v S 326. Eff 7-1-68.

§ 5731.46 County treasurer to keep account of taxes received.

The county treasurer shall keep an account showing the amount of all taxes and interest received by him under Chapter 5731. of the Revised Code. On the twenty-fifth day of February and the twentieth day of August of each year he shall settle with the county auditor for all such taxes and interest so received at the time of making such settlement, not included in any preceding settlement, showing for what estate, by whom, and when paid. At each such settlement the auditor shall allow to the treasurer and himself, on the money so collected and accounted for by him, their respective fees, at the percentages allowed by law. The correctness thereof, together with a statement of the fees allowed at such settlement, and the fees and expenses allowed to the officers under such chapter shall be certified by the auditor.

HISTORY: 132 v S 326. Eff 7-1-68.

§ 5731.47 Fees of officers; approval; payment.

The fees of the sheriff or other officers for services performed under Chapter 5731. of the Revised Code, and the expenses of the county auditor shall be certified by the county auditor by a report filed with the tax commissioner. If the tax commissioner finds that such fees and expenses are correct and reasonable in amount, he shall indicate his approval in writing to the county auditor. The auditor shall pay such fees and expenses out of the state's share of the undivided inheritance taxes in the county treasury and draw his warrants payable from such taxes, on the county treasurer in fa-

vor of the fee funds or officers personally entitled thereto.

HISTORY: 132 v S 326. Eff 7-1-68.

§ 5731.48 Distribution of tax revenues.

If a decedent dies on or after July 1, 1989, sixty-four per cent of the gross amount of taxes levied and paid under this chapter shall be for the use of the municipal corporation or township in which the tax originates, and shall be credited as follows:

(A) To the general revenue fund in the case of a city;

(B) To the general revenue fund of a village or to the board of education of a village, for school purposes, as the village council by resolution may approve;

(C) To the general revenue fund or to the board of education of the school district of which the township is a part, for school purposes, as the board of township trustees by resolution may approve, in the case of a township.

Where a municipal corporation is in default with respect to the principal or interest of any outstanding notes or bonds, one half of the taxes distributed under this section shall be credited to the sinking or bond retirement fund of the municipal corporation, and the residue shall be credited to the general revenue fund.

The council, board of trustees, or other legislative authority of a village or township may, by ordinance in the case of a village, or by resolution in the case of a township, provide that whenever there is money in the treasury of the village or township from taxes levied under this chapter, not required for immediate use, that money may be invested in federal, state, county, or municipal bonds, upon which there has been no default of the principal during the preceding five years.

The remainder of the taxes levied and paid under this chapter, after deducting the fees and costs charged against the proceeds of the tax under this chapter, shall be for the use of the state, and shall be paid into the state treasury to the credit of the general revenue fund.

HISTORY: 132 v S 326 (Eff 7-1-68); 140 v H 291 (Eff 7-1-83); 143 v H 111 (Eff 7-1-89); 144 v S 206 (Eff 6-29-91); 144 v H 298. Eff 7-26-91.

See provisions, § 127 of HB 291 (140 v —) following RC § 5731.01.

§ 5731.49 Determination of tax revenues due political subdivisions; payment.

At each semiannual settlement provided for by section 5731.46 of the Revised Code the county auditor shall certify to the county auditor of any other county in which is located in whole or in part any municipal corporation or township to which any of the taxes collected under this chapter and not previously accounted for, is due, a statement of the amount of such taxes due to each corporation or township in such county entitled to share in the distribution thereof. The amount due upon such settlement to each such municipal corporation or township, and to each municipal corporation and township in the county in which the taxes are collected, shall be paid upon the warrant of the county auditor to the county treasurer or other proper officer of such municipal corporation or township. The amount of any refund chargeable against any such municipal corporation or township at the time of making such settlement, shall be adjusted in determining the amount due to such municipal corporation or township at such settlement; provided that if the municipal corporation or township against which such refund is chargeable is not entitled to share in the fund to be distributed at such settlement, the auditor shall draw his warrant for the amount in favor of the treasurer payable from any undivided general taxes in the possession of such treasurer, unless such municipal corporation or township is located in another county, in which event the auditor shall issue a certificate for such amount to the auditor of the proper county, who shall draw a like

warrant therefor payable from any undivided general taxes in the possession of the treasurer of such county. In either case at the next semiannual settlement of such undivided general taxes, the amount of such warrant shall be deducted from the distribution of taxes of such municipal corporation or township and charged against the proceeds of levies for the general fund of such municipal corporation or township, and a similar deduction shall be made at each next semiannual settlement of such undivided general taxes until such warrant has been satisfied in full.

HISTORY: 132 v S 326 (Eff 7-1-68); 143 v H 230. Eff 10-30-89.

§ 5731.50 Origin of tax on transfer of realty and tangible personalty located in state.

When the property transferred is real estate or tangible personal property within this state, the tax on the transfer thereof shall be deemed to have originated in the municipal corporation or township in which such property is physically located. In case of real estate located in more than one municipal corporation or township, the tax on the transfer thereof, or of any interest therein, shall be apportioned between the municipal corporation or townships in which it is located in the proportions in which the tract is assessed for general property taxation in such townships or municipal corporations.

HISTORY: 132 v S 326. Eff 7-1-68.

§ 5731.51 Origin of tax on transfer of personalty not located in state.

The tax on the transfer of intangible property or tangible personal property not within this state from a resident of this state shall be deemed to have originated in the municipal corporation or township in which the decedent was domiciled.

The municipal corporation or township in which the tax on the transfer of the intangible property of a nonresident accruing under Chapter 5731. of the Revised Code shall be deemed to have originated, shall be determined as follows:

(A) As to bonds, notes, or other securities or assets, in the possession or in the control or custody of a corporation, institution, or person in this state, such tax shall be deemed to have originated in the municipal corporation or township in which such corporation, institution or person had the same in possession, control, or custody at the time of the transfer.

(B) As to money on deposit with any corporation, bank, institution, or person, such tax shall be deemed to have originated in the municipal corporation or township in which such corporation, bank or other institution had its principal place of business, or in which such person resided at the time of such succession.

HISTORY: 132 v S 326 (Eff 7-1-68); 133 v H 1. Eff 3-18-69.

§ 5731.90 Confidentiality of tax returns and other records.

(A)(1) Except as provided in division (A)(2) of this section, to the extent that any of the following are in the possession of a probate court, the department of taxation, a county auditor or county treasurer, the attorney general, or other authorized person as specified in this chapter, the following and any of their contents are confidential; are not subject to inspection or copying as public records pursuant to section 149.43 of the Revised Code; and may be inspected or copied by members of the general public only after the probate court of the county in which a return was filed pursuant to this chapter or, if none, another appropriate probate court, has issued an order, based on good cause shown, specifically authorizing the inspection or copying:

(a) An estate tax return, generation-skipping tax return, or other tax return filed pursuant to this chapter;

(b) All documents and other records that pertain to the determination of a decedent's taxable estate that is the subject of a return as described in division (A)(1)(a) of this section;

(c) The amount of the estate, generation-skipping, or other taxes paid or payable in connection with a decedent's taxable estate as described in division (A)(1)(b) of this section.

(2) Division (A)(1) of this section does not do any of the following:

(a) Preclude the inspection, copying, and use of an estate, generation-skipping, or other tax return filed pursuant to this chapter, documents and other records as described in division (A)(1)(b) of this section, and the amount of the estate, generation-skipping, or other taxes paid or payable in connection with a decedent's taxable estate as described in that division, by the tax commissioner, county auditors and treasurers, probate judges, the attorney general, and other authorized persons as specified in this chapter, in connection with their duties and responsibilities as described in this chapter, including, but not limited to, the determination and collection of an estate, generation-skipping, or other tax;

(b) Preclude the tax commissioner from furnishing to the internal revenue service, in accordance with federal law and in connection with its official business, a copy of any estate, generation-skipping, or other tax return, any document or other record, or the amount of any estate, generation-skipping, or other tax paid or payable, as described in division (A)(2)(a) of this section;

(c) Apply to the certificates described in division (A)(1)(b) of section 5731.21 of the Revised Code that, pursuant to division (A)(5) of that section, are made public records subject to inspection and copying in accordance with section 149.43 of the Revised Code;

(d) Affect rights of inspection under Chapter 1347. of the Revised Code by persons who are the subject of personal information contained in an estate, generation-skipping, or other tax return, or any document or other record, as described in division (A)(2)(a) of this section.

(B) No person shall do any of the following:

(1) Permit the inspection or copying of an estate tax return, generation-skipping tax return, or other tax return filed pursuant to this chapter, or documents and other records that pertain to the determination of the decedent's taxable estate that is the subject of the return, except as provided in division (A) of this section;

(2) Otherwise divulge information contained in the return or the documents or other records, except as provided in division (A) of this section;

(3) Divulge the amount of the estate, generation-skipping, or other taxes paid or payable in connection with the decedent's taxable estate that is the subject of the return, except as provided in division (A) of this section.

HISTORY: 143 v H 286. Eff 11-8-90.

§ 5731.99   Penalty.

Whoever violates this chapter, or any lawful rule promulgated by the tax commissioner under authority of this chapter, for the violation of which no other penalty is provided in this chapter, shall be fined not less than one hundred or more than five thousand dollars.

HISTORY: 140 v H 291. Eff 7-1-83.

See provisions, § 127 of HB 291 (140 v —) following RC § 5731.01.

INDEX

References are to sections
